G000037866

Praise for *The Self-Evolved Leader*

"Dave McKeown is a rising voice in the world of leadership. In *The Self-Evolved Leader*, he brings a fresh approach that is sorely needed in our organizations."

Marshall Goldsmith, Thinkers50 #1 Executive Coach for 10 years

"Evolving yourself as a leader is mandatory in these complex, challenging times. Dave McKeown provides easy-to-implement, simple-to-maintain techniques and strategies to modernize your leadership and ensure your team is ready for what's next."

Cy Wakeman, author of *No Ego*

"You might assume that *The Self-Evolved Leader* is just another self-help business tome. You'd be wrong. Five minutes into Dave McKeown's easy-going pages, you'll find yourself nodding along with his observations about how most leaders really behave. By the end of the book, you'll be convinced enough of Dave's wisdom to repeat his self-evolved leader's mantra daily (sorry, you have to read the book to find out). This is a warm, acute and persuasive work: If you lead a team of any size, *The Self-Evolved Leader* can help you and your team together do the best work of your lives."

Eric Schurenberg, CEO, Mansueto Ventures

"It's both embarrassing and frustrating when you discover your well-meaning attempts at heroic leadership have kept you and your team stuck in a cycle of mediocrity. You're exhausted, they're frustrated, and everyone's underperforming. Dave McKeown draws on wisdom and experience to give you the insights to break the cycle and a plan to actually change the way you lead."

Michael Bungay Stanier, bestselling author
of *The Coaching Habit*

"In a world that craves more empathy and authenticity, Dave McKeown shares a candid call to action for leaders today. I love the micro-disciplines—they are immediately applicable and will create impact for your team and business today."

Stacey Engle, President, Fierce, Inc.

"In this practical and inspirational book, Dave lays out a path to help leaders let go of the reins of heroic leadership and unleash the potential of their teams. Too many teams experience 'learned helplessness' and the cycle of mediocrity that ensues. It is challenging to get out of this cycle without clear guidance and support. In *The Self-Evolved Leader*, David provides a clear roadmap that will transform your leadership and the performance of your team. Read it and put these wise words into practice!"

Julie Wilson, Founder and Executive Director,
Institute for the Future of Learning

"You were driven enough to get to this point in your business. But drive alone will not get you to the next level. *The Self-Evolved Leader* provides the practical knowledge and a precise roadmap to become the leader your business needs in the future."

Jim Murray, President, A.K. Rikk's

"*The Self-Evolved Leader* is a practical yet provocative guide to leading in an ever-changing world. It's a good reminder to continually challenge your approach and way of thinking and to remember that what got you here isn't necessarily what is going to get you there. I highly recommend reading it and sharing it with everyone on your team."

Dawn Conway, CEO, Boost Engagement

"Leadership is not 'diving catches and acts of heroism.' Instead, it's about something very different. In this book, Dave McKeown unpacks the lessons he's learned from organizations and leaders to give you the tools, strategies, and inspiration to develop a new style of leadership so that you can become the kind of person who can lead in a world that refuses to slow down. Rarely have I seen a book that's as practical as this one. I changed my own leadership style for the better as a direct result of reading it.

The Self-Evolved Leader is hands-on inspiration for leaders at all levels who know that old-school leadership doesn't work anymore. The secret? Don't just read it! Follow Dave's advice about what to try at the end of each chapter. I've known Dave for years and have always admired his approach to life. This book successfully encapsulates his maverick perspective in a way that accurately reflects what's required of leaders today. This book is a game changer for anyone who believes leadership needs to look different in today's changing world."

Jeb Brooks, CEO, The Brooks Group

"Dave McKeown continues to deliver! Having worked with Dave over a span of two decades *The Self Evolved Leader* is another work of art Dave has built to develop leaders. The applications in his book are real, practical, and provide a step-by-step playbook on how to win as a leader!"

Al Carlson, VP of HR, Talent Management,
and Leadership Development, BTD

"*The Self-Evolved Leader* is written for anyone that aspires to be a leader at any level. It's a powerful yet essential and easy to use playbook, built upon Dave McKeown's exceptional track record for coaching and inspiring others to aim higher. His passion for getting to the heart of what makes a great leader really shines through. A must-read!"

Traci Wilk, Senior VP People, The Learning Experience

THE
SELF-EVOLVED
LEADER

Elevate Your Focus and
Develop Your People in a World
That Refuses to Slow Down

Dave McKeown

GREENLEAF
BOOK GROUP PRESS

This publication is designed to provide accurate and authoritative information in regard to the subject matter covered. It is sold with the understanding that the publisher and author are not engaged in rendering legal, accounting, or other professional services. Nothing herein shall create an attorney-client relationship, and nothing herein shall constitute legal advice or a solicitation to offer legal advice. If legal advice or other expert assistance is required, the services of a competent professional should be sought.

Additionally, persons and businesses referenced in this book may be composites, thus references to any real persons or businesses are not implied.

Published by Greenleaf Book Group Press
Austin, Texas
www.gbgpress.com

Copyright ©2020 Dave McKeown

All rights reserved.

Thank you for purchasing an authorized edition of this book and for complying with copyright law. No part of this book may be reproduced, stored in a retrieval system, or transmitted by any means, electronic, mechanical, photocopying, recording, or otherwise, without written permission from the copyright holder.

Distributed by Greenleaf Book Group

For ordering information or special discounts for bulk purchases, please contact Greenleaf Book Group at PO Box 91869, Austin, TX 78709, 512.891.6100.

Design and composition by Greenleaf Book Group
Cover design by Greenleaf Book Group
Cover Images: ©iStockphoto.com/Wiyada Arunwaikit
Author Photography by Elliot O'Donovan

Publisher's Cataloging-in-Publication data is available.

Print ISBN: 978-1-62634-680-2

eBook ISBN: 978-1-62634-681-9

Part of the Tree Neutral® program, which offsets the number of trees consumed in the production and printing of this book by taking proactive steps, such as planting trees in direct proportion to the number of trees used: www.treeneutral.com

TreeNeutral

Printed in the United States of America on acid-free paper

19 20 21 22 23 24   10 9 8 7 6 5 4 3 2 1

First Edition

To Paris.
Without you this would not exist.

Contents

What Came Before Is No Longer Enough

E ach year we spend tens of billions of dollars on leadership training, books, workshops, webinars, coaches, and keynote speeches. Despite the colossal amount we invest in building better leaders, we're experiencing a more significant leadership gap than ever before.

Employee motivation is at an all-time low, turnover is up, and in survey after survey, the gulf between leaders' self-assessments of their effectiveness and the perception by those whom they lead is ever expanding.

This is important for two reasons. First, the world we live in isn't getting any less complex; we aren't going to return to a simpler time. For you, as a leader, the requirement to get more from your team with fewer resources is only going to get more acute.

Second, the problems faced by our organizations, communities, and species aren't going to get any easier. Climate change, rising income inequality, the polarization of our political discourse, and the lens of tribalism through which we view the best way to tackle our most significant challenges all require a cadre of leaders who will rise to help us find a better way through—together. Never before have we needed a generation of leaders to step up and lead with authenticity, purpose, and effectiveness as urgently as we do now.

This book aims to provide a road map for leaders at any level of any organization to discover their authentic leadership calling, create a vision of a better world, and build the framework and structure needed to chart the course.

The Challenges for Leaders Today

Since the industrial revolution, we've been pursuing an elusive model of leadership that often seems within our grasp, only to find it slip through our hands like sand. Part of that is because the world around us is changing so quickly, and part of it is because we rely too heavily on our past successes to define our models of the future. The problem is that in a world of "unknown unknowns," our requirements for effective leadership change faster than the most recent fad.

We're stuck between two worlds. On one hand, we're barely starting to move away from the old, industrial-era way of thinking about leadership and its relentless focus on top-down hierarchy and planning, which by many accounts succeeded in driving shareholder value but stripped out employee motivation, value, and satisfaction. On the other hand, we haven't fully developed our thoughts on what comes after the bureaucratic organization. The democratization of technology has allowed us to experiment with new models of working that emphasize decentralization of autonomy and decision making and seek to increase employee ownership. Coupled with this trend, we've seen a shift in the cultural zeitgeist toward a more mindful way of working and leading that emphasizes the individual rather than the employee, but our metamorphosis is incomplete.

We're now operating in limbo, understanding that what

worked before will not necessarily work forever but unsure of what the next iteration of our organizations looks like. As a result, you, as a leader, have to operate in the void between these two worlds, helping to navigate your team through this journey.

In my work coaching leadership teams and individuals, I see this dynamic has created a rising tide of issues. As a leader, you can choose to ignore these issues or tackle them head-on. Doing so requires adopting a different perspective, a different approach, and a set of disciplines you may not be comfortable with. It requires you to lay down the old ways of thinking about leadership and to take a step toward being a Self-Evolved Leader.

The Need to Balance Agility with Execution

We talk a lot about the need to stay agile, to move with our customers, to be aware of industry trends and changing demographics. However, every time we make a shift in strategy or direction, we lose our focus on execution. It's almost a zero-sum game. For every response, we lose a bit of traction; and for every period of implementation, we miss out on the opportunity to respond. Self-Evolved Leaders know how to balance the tension between these two extremes to move to a position of executing and evaluating the need for change at the same time.

Achieving More with Fewer Resources

It's no secret that in many organizations budgets are getting squeezed; the need to add more to the bottom line with fewer people is increasing. We're spinning more and more plates, and it's leading to stress, exhaustion, and burnout.

Self-Evolved Leaders know how to take a breath and not rush to action but actively seek to get the best from their team without overburdening them. They know how to create a culture where people want to give their discretionary effort to move the team forward. They're working smarter and harder, and they're enjoying every minute of it.

A Constant Pull on Our Attention

If you've made it this far into the book in one sitting without being pulled away by another distraction, then congratulations, you've already read more pages of a book than most adults will today!

We're living in a world of constant bombardment, of relentless communication and the possibility that anyone can interrupt us at any time. Our brains are literally getting rewired to respond to the stimulus of interruption.

The Self-Evolved Leader has developed the ability to focus for extended periods on the work that matters without getting pulled away by constant distraction.

A Changing Workplace

The makeup of our society, and in turn our workplaces, is shifting more quickly and in more meaningful ways than in any point in history. We're embracing more cultural, generational, and gender diversity than before. As a result, old power structures are crumbling and we're building a more inclusive workplace. The challenge lies in creating an organizational culture that embraces and celebrates this diversity in a way that allows us to achieve our common goals.

The Self-Evolved Leader knows how to get the best from their team regardless of age, tenure at the company, or any other demographic factors by embracing a diversity of thought and pushing for the best outcome for the team, organization, and community no matter who is involved in the decision-making process.

Where Other Models Fail

Many good, even great leadership models have come before this one that have inspired those before you to become effective leaders. Many, also, have their DNA sprinkled throughout the core principles of *The Self-Evolved Leader*. I owe my entire career and the life that I hold so dear to those past models.

However, as Marshall Goldsmith, one of the top leadership coaches, says, "What got you here won't get you there." Where many of the books fail and where the media has done us a disservice is in pushing the following leadership fallacies.

Overemphasis on the Visionary Leader

Too often our role models for leadership are the visionaries who completely reimagine a product, an industry, or the world: Jobs, Musk, Bezos, Zuckerberg, Mandela, Oprah. The problem with this approach is that most visionary leaders are born with the risk-taking and creative mind-set needed to achieve their feats of greatness. Sure, they learned to hone their craft over time and had a bit of luck to boot, but most of us weren't born to be wild risk takers. The overemphasis on the side hustle, on pursuing your passion, has created the belief that anyone can and should be an entrepreneur—that it's the only route to true fulfillment.

When you use that as your exemplar of great leadership, you get too many people leading in a way that isn't natural to them. In doing so, they use leadership as an excuse to be a tyrant, to push too hard, and at extremes to lie, cheat, and steal their way to success.

Yes, we need visionary leaders, and if it's your natural proclivity to push the boundaries of what's possible and truly reimagine a new world, then keep doing that. The lessons in *The Self-Evolved Leader* will dramatically accelerate your effectiveness.

For those who aren't that way inclined, however, that's OK. There is plenty of room for leaders who are less focused on pushing the boundaries and more likely to press for evolution rather than revolution. These are the leaders who will help navigate the change so badly needed in our organizations and who will ultimately build a legacy on the impact they leave on the people they work with and serve every day.

So, dispel the myth that you somehow need to be an entrepreneurial mastermind to be a great leader. There are many other routes to get there, as you'll discover throughout this book.

Reliance on Heroics

Closely linked to the false model of the visionary leader is an overreliance on heroics. We've heard time and again in movies, literature, and sports of the lonely hero who embarked on a personal journey of discovery and managed to steal victory from the jaws of defeat, save the day, and emerge transformed.

These mythical stories have infiltrated their way into our perception of an effective leader. Yes, there are times when we need diving catches and acts of heroism, but if that's what your success as a team or organization is built on, then you have a shaky foundation. There are only so many superheroes you can hire.

Instead, it's more sustainable to build a foundation of great leadership that's based on shared accountability rather than heroics. Building deep ownership allows your team to have flurries of heroism, without the heroics becoming the defining feature.

Focus on Singular Outward Behaviors

Most leadership models out there focus on an output, action, or behavior. If only you could tackle difficult conversations better, you'd be a stronger leader. If you could get a handle on your time management, you could get more done. Changing an action or behavior is, after all, the end goal of any leadership shift. The problem lies in the fact that focusing on changing a single behavior without having a deep understanding of who you are as a leader is equivalent to taking your car into the garage for a paint job when the engine needs replacing. Over the long run, it's hard for that behavior to stick.

Rather than focusing on individual behaviors in isolation, it's more effective to look at how those behaviors are interconnected, which of them are most important in helping you and your team achieve your goals, and where your biggest strengths and development points lie.

Development through Osmosis

Certain people are born to be leaders. For everybody else, however, there's a belief that the only real way to grow and develop is to somehow put yourself in enough challenging situations that you'll pick up the right and the wrong way to do things. Either that or you can read a book, go to a workshop, or listen to a keynote and somehow, by osmosis, you'll become a better leader. That's like saying you'll become a better runner by listening to someone talk about their victory in the New York City Marathon.

We talk about leadership as a "soft" skill: one that's hard to train or develop due to its intangible nature. When we do that, we get "soft" leadership. Instead, we should view it as a hard-edged skill that can be worked on, practiced, and ultimately mastered—no different than playing an instrument or learning to code or taking up dance lessons. Through sheer hard work, grit, and determination you can become a more effective, more authentic leader in a much shorter period of time than you'd think. You just need a guide to get there.

Who Is This Book For?

If you're anything like me, when you're in the mood for a new book, you pick the most interesting-sounding one, skim through the introduction to get the key points, flip to a few other pages, look at the testimonials, and determine if there's anything new, relevant, or interesting in there for you before you either buy it or set it down.

One of my guiding principles in the workshops I deliver is for the participants to take what's useful and leave the rest. You are responsible for your own learning and development. And so, while I'd be honored if you bought a copy of this book, if it's not right for you at all or now is just not the right time, that's great too.

With that said, my goal and desire is to get a copy into as many hands as possible. I truly believe the perspectives and lessons in here will help us build toward the leadership revolution we sorely need. To that end, I wrote it to be as accessible and useful to as broad a range of readers as possible. As I see it, there are three specific groups who will derive benefit from reading it.

Individuals

Primarily this book is for you, no matter what your leadership position, industry, or geography may be. Change in your people, in the way you lead, and ultimately in your organization comes down to the capability of you as the individual leader. As Robert Anderson and William Adams said in *Mastering Leadership*,

"The organization will never perform at a higher level than the consciousness of its leadership." At times it may feel challenging to push the boundaries of your leadership within the overarching culture of your organization, and so the purpose of this book is to provide you with a model to follow that will set you apart as a Self-Evolved Leader.

Whether you're a C-level executive who has been in leadership for most of your adult life, or you've just gotten your first management role and you're eager to make the most significant impact you can in the shortest period of time, the advice, guidance, and wisdom in these pages have been written to inspire you to become the best version of yourself, and to provide you with the necessary tools to get there.

Teams

Sharing a common language and vocabulary around great leadership, communication, decision making, and accountability is the catalyst that unlocks team performance. It's the difference between a *good* team and a *great* team.

The principles in this book are primarily born from my work with senior leadership teams in fast-growing organizations. I hope that as you read this, you will share it with your leadership team and adopt the language and models in this book as your catalyst for success.

Organizations

Large-scale change in organizations is hard. The way we've succeeded historically has such a stronghold over our definitions of culture and leadership that we cling tightly to old methods and ways of thinking.

This book is a clarion call to adopt new ways of thinking and to integrate those into your organization as a whole. The more widely you can disseminate the principles and utilize some of the routines and rituals, the more effective, collaborative, and innovative you'll see your organization become and the bigger impact it will have on your community.

How Is the Book Structured?

The Self-Evolved Leader was written to take you on a journey, from making the critical shift in perspective needed to break the cycle of mediocre leadership, to building a foundation for effective leadership, strengthening the disciplines you need to deliver great leadership, and ending with a plan for mastering and sustaining leadership.

It is split into four main parts.

PART 1:
Preparing for Self-Evolved Leadership

All transformations start with an understanding that the old way of thinking no longer works in our current context. The first section of *The Self-Evolved Leader* lays out the argument that for too long, leaders have been walking around with an incorrect assumption about the value they add to their organization, namely, that their role is to be the hero, save the day, make the diving catches, and move from crisis to crisis putting out fires.

Part 1 explores the folly of this mind-set and how it establishes a dangerous cycle of mediocrity between you and your team. It then lays out the most crucial perspective shift you need to make to become a Self-Evolved Leader, that your value comes not from saving the day but from equipping your people to deliver on the day-to-day tactics and grow into the best version of themselves so that you can focus on the medium- and long-term direction of your team.

PART 2:
The Key Elements of Self-Evolved Leadership

Once you've committed to break the cycle of mediocre leadership and have hit reset with your team, the second part of the book lays out the key elements for developing Self-Evolved Leadership.

Specifically, it shares how you can create a compelling vision to inspire your team, then build a pulse for implementation, and ultimately develop the key disciplines to sharpen your focus and elevate your people.

PART 3:
Mastering the Self-Evolved Leadership Disciplines

This section of the book is a deep dive into five key leadership disciplines, each interconnected and necessary to compete in today's fast-moving environment. Rather than approaching each discipline as a skill, or even a set of skills, this section lays out the rituals and practices you can implement in your day-to-day leadership to ensure you're working toward mastery.

PART 4:
Sustaining Self-Evolved Leadership

An old mentor of mine once told me that "the distance between being good and being great is a mile wide and a micron thick." It means that when you get good at something, the jump to greatness doesn't seem to be a bridge too far; you can see it, but it still requires a lot of work to get there. Unfortunately, most people decide to stay at the point of good enough rather than pushing forward to greatness.

Part 4 of this book is about pushing through that final yard or two toward greatness. In this section you will discover a process for ingraining the philosophies and practices of the Self-Evolved Leader into your daily interactions, as well as a model for introducing what you're learning into the rest of the organization.

How to Use This Book

Rather than being a list of leadership platitudes or philosophies, this book is intended to be your instruction manual, your playbook for getting the most out of yourself, your team, and your organization.

To that end, the best way to use the book is to start at the beginning and work through it in chronological order. Each chapter builds on the next, taking you a step forward in your leadership journey. It's been written in a way that it could be consumed in one sitting; however, you may want to take more time with it. Whatever pace is right for you, I suggest you start at the beginning and work your way through, rather than jumping to a chapter that seems interesting.

What You Can Expect to Achieve

Whether you work through this book individually or as a team, if you're diligent and take the opportunity to integrate the principles, routines, and practices in your leadership, I can guarantee you'll discover that:

- You're able to get more done in less time.

- You'll stop managing from crisis to crisis and will spend more time focusing on the medium- and long-term development of your people.

- You'll get better results from your team.

- You'll dramatically increase the value you bring and the impact you have on your organization and community.

Ready to get started? Let's get stuck in!

PART 1

Preparing for
Self-Evolved Leadership

1

Break the Cycle of Mediocrity

"**S**orry, Dave. I have to take this; it's Steve." Jen snatched her phone and stood up from the hefty desk we were sitting at and moved toward the corner window.

"Hey, Steve. What's up?" she said as she plugged in her headset.

I thought back to when we started working together six months before. Jen had just been promoted to vice president of sales and marketing in a fast-growing tech company. Her rise through the ranks had been somewhat meteoric, and she was trying to come to terms with the responsibilities of her new role.

"OK, well, tell Eric I'll call him this afternoon. Don't worry, Steve. We'll fix this."

I knew by the look on her face that she meant "I'll fix this."

Jen moved back toward the table and set the phone down.

"Something up?" I asked. We both knew it was a leading question.

"That customer I was telling you about is just about to pull their business, and Steve needs me to put in a call to their purchasing guy to smooth things over."

"*Needs* you to?" I asked. Jen shot me a look.

"Listen, Dave." She moved toward me. "I know you've been helping me try to elevate my focus and not get in the weeds so much, but this is a full-blown crisis."

I leaned back and put my hands up to signal that I wasn't about to criticize the work she'd been doing.

"I completely understand that. Sounds as though you might have a genuine emergency on your hands," I said. "Tell me, what has Steve done so far to try to keep the account?"

Jen sighed with a degree of resignation, then gritted her teeth. "I don't know, Dave," she said without seeming to move her jaw. "I didn't ask him."

"So, what's your best outcome here?"

"Well, I guess I'll call Eric, do my best to assuage his fears, and get him back on board."

"And Steve? What does he take away from this?"

Jen shut her eyes, I think somewhat hoping that when she opened them, I'd be gone. "I get it, OK. I've just done that thing. What do you call it?"

"Built learned helplessness?"

"Yeah, that's the one. Agghh, I hate when I do that. I've just gone back on the very first transition that we talked about, right? I'm getting pulled back into heroic leadership."

"It's OK!" I said, adopting a conciliatory tone. "Don't beat yourself up. It happens all the time. Do you need to take a moment?"

"Yeah, let me call Steve back and see what he can do. Do you mind?"

"Not at all. I'll go make myself a cup of coffee and meet you back here in fifteen."

The Cycle of Mediocrity

Jen, like so many other leaders before her, had fallen into a misguided way of thinking: that her value as a leader was found in her ability to fix things, to make the diving catches and save the day. Unfortunately, we've allowed a distorted image of what it means to lead to enter our organizations, and it's causing a profound and dangerous knock-on effect on our teams. Let's call it the Cycle of Mediocrity.

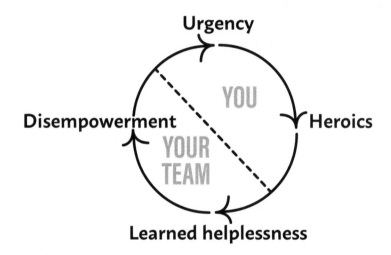

Urgency and Heroic Leadership

The growing complexity of our world and the speed at which things change and information is communicated have falsely led us to believe that it's quicker and easier to act and act now rather than taking a moment to review the best course of action. So, when our largest customer is about to pull their business, we'll get on the phone to our contact and save the day rather than getting our team involved. When our boss asks for the updated status report two days before it's due, we pull an all-nighter to get it done instead of assessing the true urgency. When one of our team makes a simple mistake on this month's financials, we fix it rather than sending it back with some feedback. We've allowed every input into our daily routine to become "urgent" and spend most of our time stuck fighting fires and lurching from crisis to crisis rather than affording ourselves the headspace to think about what's important—the long-term direction of our team and the development of our people. We're leading through acts of heroism.

This has been amplified by the fact that we have an ever-increasing list of role models for good leadership that are centered on the role of the hero. We're bombarded with examples of heroes who save the day, from sports to the military to mythology.

These enigmatic figures pull victory from the jaws of defeat, they make the diving catches, they embark on a quest with a reluctant hope and emerge from their journey transformed. They may bring a team *along* with them, but without a standout quarterback throwing a Hail Mary or Captain America swooping in at the last minute, we all lose.

The problem is that none of these spheres are analogous to a growing organization. They come with their own rules and their own parameters for success. We don't get to see what happens to the hero's life once the final image of them in all their sweat, blood, and triumph fades away.

However, in the absence of a direct comparison, we've subconsciously translated our notion of the heroic leader from the worlds of sports, the military, and mythology to a corporate setting, and it isn't pretty. We've lauded our workplace heroes and presented them with their own superpowers and, as a result, more and more leaders embody the following characteristics.

They Swing for the Fences

Heroic leaders say "yes" and then figure out how to deliver what they just agreed to do through brute force. For the heroic leader, getting the job done and satisfying the customer is almost more important than what the job is itself, and certainly more important than the impact it has on their team.

What happens then is that they say yes to a myriad of things and then have their team scramble like crazy underneath to make the whole thing come together. That's not leadership. That's throwing spaghetti at a wall, seeing what sticks, and then having your team clean up the mess.

They Confuse Busyness with Progress

Heroic leaders surround themselves in a dust cloud of activity, running from meeting to meeting, phone call to phone call, and watercooler conversation to networking event with nary a heartbeat to actually sit down and think through the decisions they're making on any given day.

They hold the belief that as long as we continue to move in a direction, any direction, we're making progress. In the wake of the leader's busyness, however, they leave their team without clear direction, assuming that the team will magically understand their thoughts by sheer osmosis.

They Believe They Have the Answers

Anytime a team member approaches the heroic leader with a problem to be solved or a challenge that needs to be overcome, this type of leader instantly and without breath knows the right course of action to take (even if it isn't the best decision) and quickly provides advice to unwitting team members like a Pez dispenser.

Heroic leaders believe that they are in the position they are in precisely because of this approach. It's a feature, not a bug. As a result, their team becomes more and more reliant on the heroic leader to help them out of tricky situations.

They Save the Day

"I'll deal with it." The heroic leader's favorite phrase. They view themselves not as the blocker and tackler for their team but as the quarterback throwing the Hail Mary. Why bother helping a team member devise a plan of action when it would take the heroic leader half the time to complete it and probably have it work out twice as successfully? Also, as this leader would be thinking, *Let's face it, I'll probably have to jump in and fix it at some point anyway.*

It's not that heroic leaders are bad people. Most have good, if not great, intentions, but they find themselves in an almost addictive feedback loop. Each time we exhibit acts of heroism, we get a small dopamine hit that makes us feel valued, useful, and needed. We then start to (albeit subconsciously) seek out those opportunities. As a result, we begin to treat every interruption as an emergency, which in turn gives us an opportunity to get that hit of dopamine. Before you know it, we've found ourselves caught in an endless cycle of treating everything like a crisis that only we can solve.

Heroic leadership in your organization doesn't have to happen in bold, sweeping ways to be harmful. You don't have to embody all the characteristics listed above to be guilty of it. It can be as simple as saying something like, "Don't worry, I've got it." Or, "Leave that there, I'll deal with it." With every small drip of heroism, you're further crippling the effectiveness of your team. In fact, you're building learned helplessness within them.

Learned Helplessness

In 1974, Martin Seligman, then a researcher at the University of Pennsylvania, and his colleagues sought to understand how humans react to unpleasant environments that appear beyond their control. In an experiment, they separated human subjects into three groups: One was subjected to an awful noise that they could control by pressing a button four times, the second experienced the same terrible din but the button they were given didn't work, and the third heard no noise.

A little later, after the ear-ringing had subsided, the participants were all subjected to another obnoxious sound, but this time they had a lever rather than a button at their disposal to control it. Seligman and his associates found that those from the group with no control over their environment earlier that day, in general, did not try to use the lever to turn off the noise, while everyone else more or less managed to figure it out.

Seligman concluded that when faced with a situation over which you have no control, that feeling embeds itself cognitively and becomes an accepted truth. Even when things appear to have changed around you, your desire to change your circumstances decreases, and in turn, it can lead to a sense of depression. These subjects had developed learned helplessness.

I hate to break it to you, but most of your team has likely developed some form of learned helplessness from your acts of heroism. Not of the loud noise variety, but something much more subtle yet equally dangerous. In being an overwhelmed leader who is taking on too much and trying to save the day, you reinforce the belief that your team isn't quite good enough, that it requires something special or magical from you to make it just so. That in itself puts a brake on your team's desire to go above and beyond what's necessary, and instead to sit back and wait for you to bail them out. It's by no means malicious, nor is it likely to be what your team wants to happen. In fact, most of them probably don't even realize they're doing it when they are.

Disempowerment and Feeling Overwhelmed

In the long run, learned helplessness leads to disempowerment. Over time your team slowly cedes authority to you. They subconsciously elect not to make a tough call, so as to defer to your wisdom, to give you the final say.

You'll notice that some on your team will willingly let this happen. For them, they feel more comfortable having someone else bear that load. For others, however, it's more frustrating. They feel that the value they bring begins to erode. They may even resist initially, but as you continue to lead through heroics, eventually they too will start to give up all but the most basic aspects of their role. They end up disempowered.

This leads to a feeling of resentment on your part. Where you used to feel that your team or certainly individual members within it had a degree of ownership over what they did, now it seems they've lost their edge. Maybe they too are overwhelmed, you think. But not as overwhelmed as you.

For as you take on more and more of the authority they cede to you, coupled with an unrelenting influx of new projects and initiatives from around the organization, you start to cripple under the weight of the work you have to take on. You start to build resentment toward your team, and you begin to move from being the hero in all this to being the victim. You're beginning to burn out.

You think, if only someone was willing to step forward and take some ownership for their own actions, then not only would they succeed personally but you'd have some pressure lifted from your plate.

By this stage, however, it's too late, and you've already built a pattern of behavior for both yourself and your team that has squashed any opportunity for accountability.

And the Cycle Continues

Operating in the Cycle of Mediocrity keeps your focus almost exclusively in the weeds of the tactics and actions that take place every day. It's as if each day when you walk into work, your sole purpose is to survive the onslaught of fires and crises for that one day, only to find you have to do it all over again tomorrow.

Rarely, if ever, do you get to focus on the quarterly and annual horizons, on the long-term direction of your team, or on the development of your people. When you do, it's usually haphazard, unprepared, and quite often only a drive-by to get through the meeting and back to the "actual work" you have to do.

And with that, the Cycle of Mediocrity rolls on. It's not that you and your team aren't achieving things; you will likely still have moments of glorious success. But guess how they're achieved? Through sheer force and effort.

It's more that it feels you're losing your collective edge. There's a sense that the glory days of the past are gone, and as much as you'd like to return there, you know that isn't likely. You need to move forward, but you're not quite sure to where.

There Is Hope!

The good news is, there's a way to break out of the Cycle of Mediocrity, with a new set of patterns and behaviors that move toward a new cycle, the Cycle of Excellence.

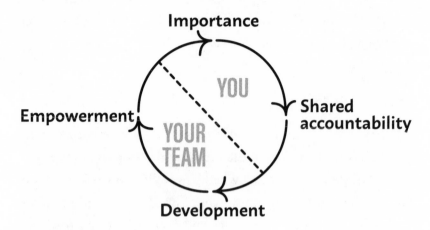

Importance

Self-Evolved Leaders recognize the dangers of constantly living in the urgent, avoiding the lure of the endorphin rush that comes with acts of heroism. Specifically, they start from the understanding that the value they bring as a leader is helping their team to stay focused on the important: the medium- and long-term direction that their team is moving toward.

Self-Evolved Leaders purposefully wall off their attention and give themselves the headspace to think in terms of the important rather than the urgent. They operate like the flow-control valves for their team, ensuring an appropriate and necessary flow of information in, around, and out from their team.

In doing so, they give themselves and their team the time they need to evaluate the best course of action, rather than rushing to acts of derring-do. At times it doesn't have to be longer than a breath, and it certainly doesn't need to bring things to a standstill. In fact, the Self-Evolved Leader has the ability to create the illusion of slowing things down at a micro level while everything around them continues to speed by.

Shared Accountability

Now that our Self-Evolved Leader has elevated their focus to the important, rather than the urgent, they're better served to assign real priority to new inputs, projects, and problems and to not rush to action. This allows them to focus on building the concept of shared accountability within their team.

Rather than relying on their own actions for success, the Self-Evolved Leader looks to their team to help define the challenges, assess solutions, and move toward a path of action.

Instead of following those old models of leadership and relentlessly carving a path in the hope that their team will follow, the Self-Evolved Leader pushes the decision-making authority deep into their team. They view their role not as the all-seeing, all-knowing swashbuckler, but instead they help their team evaluate the situation from all angles and then assist in removing obstacles to keep the entire group focused on delivering excellent work.

The resultant cultural shift is toward each team member understanding the connectedness between one another and the specific role each plays. They share the commitment that the team's success and the development of its component parts are more important than individual displays of greatness. The locus of control moves from within the leader to within the team.

Development

Moving toward shared accountability is a difficult transition to make. It involves not only breaking out of the desire to focus on the urgent but also requires a rebuilding of trust between the team and leader and likely within members of the team itself.

As we'll see in later chapters, rebuilding that trust involves treating your team as if they will succeed, and using each success and failure to help them find the lessons they need to continue to grow and develop, rather than compensating for their weaknesses. When you do this, you'll see that your team starts to develop in two ways.

First, as you give them more and more decision-making authority and responsibility, you'll discover that some members of your team will grow through the experience of handling the increasingly more complex challenges and problems you give them.

Second, as you're able to elevate your focus toward the important, you'll find yourself with more time to have conversations focused on team members' development and more clarity to assess their individual challenges.

Empowerment

The two-pronged approach of pushing decision-making authority deep into your team and helping them develop over the long run forms two sides of the same coin: *empowerment.*

In this case, empowerment is no more than the institutionalization of shared accountability and a pursuit of development in your team. It's the equivalent of removing the training wheels when teaching a child to ride a bike.

You'll know you've arrived when your team starts to have meetings without the need for your involvement, when problems get solved before you even hear about them, and when you see members of your team pushing for their own growth and development.

At this stage, you're left almost exclusively with an elevated focus on the important: the medium- and long-term direction of your team and the development of your people.

You'll notice that your team is able to get more done in less time, a sense of purpose and direction has been restored, and morale will be at the highest levels you've seen for a while. How you get there, then, is the big question. The answer to that and much more can be found in the rest of this book.

WHAT TO REMEMBER

- Heroic leadership in the long run disempowers your team.

- Your goal should be to elevate your focus to the important, not the urgent.

- Building shared accountability and focusing on developing your people moves your team toward excellence.

WHAT TO TRY

- Be mindful of moments you rush to acts of heroism.

- Keep a journal for a week and note down those moments, how you responded, and how it felt.

- Talk with your team about the Cycle of Mediocrity and Cycle of Excellence. Have an open discussion on where and when they see those behaviors emerging.

Go to the webpage below for a video summary of this chapter and other exclusive resources:

Selfevolvedleader.com/Chapter-1

2

Reset Your Perspective on Leadership

"Hey, Dave," Jen said.

"Well, how did it go?" I asked, switching my phone to speaker.

"Dave," and she paused, "it went better than I could have even imagined."

"That's great," I responded with genuine happiness. "What happened?"

Jen had just come out of an annual planning session with her team. It was a culmination of the work I'd been doing with her over the past twelve months.

"It just felt as though the team was really jiving," she said excitedly. "They led the session, the discussion was robust, everybody was engaged and enthused, and we had complete clarity on next actions."

"Wonderful, and how was your role?" I asked.

"Exactly as we had prepped for. I engaged when I needed and helped unlock a few tricky discussions, but for the most part, I just sat back and watched it all unfold."

"And what do you think the key difference was?" I probed further.

"I think I've just become more aware over the past few months. More aware of the impact I have on my team, more aware of what I can and can't control, and more aware of those moments I'm getting pulled back toward heroics." She continued, "But more than that, I think the work I've been doing with the team has reinjected trust and, I guess, the sense of empowerment that had been missing. As soon as I stopped rushing in to save the day and started trying to pull it out of them, they started to respond positively."

"Awesome, so what's next?"

"Well, now we implement. I'm so excited to see what this team is capable of this year. I think we're going to do some great things."

Watching Jen's progress over that twelve-month period was a case study in Self-Evolved Leadership. From being unable to get out of her own way to becoming one of the most mature leaders I had worked with, she serves as a valuable lesson that anyone can do it.

To get there, however, she had to learn that she needed to reset her approach to leadership. That in order to move forward she had to break down her preconceived notions of what it meant to be a great leader. Over time she started to adopt the behaviors and characteristics of the Self-Evolved Leader, both of which are worth a deeper look before we move on to the key elements in the journey to get there.

The Internal Characteristics of Self-Evolved Leaders

Every transformation starts from within, and this one is no different. Before you can make a material impact on your team and organization, there are some internal characteristics that need to be nurtured. Some of these may come naturally, and some will take a bit more time to develop.

1. They Push for Growth

At its core, Self-Evolved Leadership starts with your personal commitment. No amount of training or coaching will enable your evolution unless and until you're willing to engage in the introspection required and hard work needed to navigate the journey.

The pursuit of lifelong learning is a crucial component to growing as a Self-Evolved Leader. Lacking the desire to learn makes it almost impossible to grow past a certain point. It hurts to see so many older leaders closed off to the idea of learning, doubled down on what they've achieved to date. Conversely, too many young leaders emerge into the workplace with a sense of arrogance that comes with their newfound position.

Those leaders who push for growth know that there is still much to learn, no matter their tenure or success, and that only they are responsible for that learning. There are three defining behaviors in the Self-Evolved Leader's push for growth.

THEY PURSUE AN OBJECTIVE UNDERSTANDING OF THEIR LEADERSHIP EFFECTIVENESS

Pushing for growth in your own leadership means being open to shining the light on all aspects of your leadership—the good and the bad, the successes and the failures. It means seeking feedback from people who won't necessarily sing your praises, and pushing your team to give you the cold, unabashed truth about how they see you as a leader.

As Carol Dweck writes in her excellent book *Mindset: The New Psychology of Success*, "If, like those with the growth mindset, you believe you can develop yourself, then you're open to accurate information about your current abilities, even if it's unflattering."

A funny thing happens as you move past the initial fear of taking this approach. First off, you take the brave step of asking for feedback, your heartbeat elevates, you clench as you wait for it, and you try as much as you can to accept it for what it is rather than react with defensiveness. Then you realize it wasn't all that bad and in fact was potentially quite helpful.

Over time you start to seek out objective feedback on how you can improve. The good stuff bores you, you know that side of things anyway, and there's no learning in it. You want the stuff you can actually work on, the areas of your leadership that you can improve. That's where the real gold lies. And who knows, over time, you may even begin to enjoy receiving developmental feedback.

THEY TAKE RESPONSIBILITY FOR THEIR DEVELOPMENT

Self-Evolved Leaders put themselves in positions to learn, they seek out opportunities to grow, and they are ruthless in their pursuit to uncover the one or two takeaways for development in every opportunity they find themselves in.

It's important to note that this doesn't mean they operate from the position of greenness and naïveté of a doe-eyed student starting off their academic career seeking to soak up everything they can. Far from it; Self-Evolved Leaders develop a laser-like focus on the areas they need to work on. They adopt the old adage from Alcoholics Anonymous and other support groups to "take what you need and leave the rest." In doing so, they put themselves fully in control of their development, rather than waiting for other factors.

THEY FOCUS ON PRACTICE AND REFLECTION

More than simply taking the opportunity to learn, Self-Evolved Leaders know that in order to see their takeaways come to fruition, they have to put them into practice and assess their progress. They feel comfortable taking the risk of a different approach with their team, or to test out a new ritual or process or discipline.

Coupled with that practice, they give themselves the time to reflect on the impact they're having, to adjust their approach as necessary, and to double down when they see their new strategies are having a positive impact. All of which closes the loop on their push for growth with a renewed and still objective understanding of their leadership effectiveness.

2. They Demonstrate Vulnerability

Second in importance to a pursuit of growth and learning is to acknowledge vulnerability. In fact, it could be argued that you can't have a pursuit of lifelong learning without vulnerability. Of all the characteristics of the Self-Evolved Leader, this is the hardest to adopt. It runs antithetically to how we've been conditioned to believe we should operate in the workplace.

We've been told our whole lives that our leaders are brave, they are sure, they are steadfast. They know the answers and show the way, and we follow. Any notion of vulnerability is a sign of weakness; emotion is unprofessional; uncertainty should be avoided. That approach is a relic, I'm afraid, from our belief in heroic leadership. Yet it's become ingrained in how we show up every day.

Self-Evolved Leaders take the opposite approach. They view vulnerability as a great strength. They adopt the perspective from University of Houston research professor and author Brené Brown that "Vulnerability is not weakness. It's the most accurate measurement of courage."

Without vulnerability you can't have an objective understanding of your leadership effectiveness. Without vulnerability you can't build shared accountability. Without vulnerability you can't build a collective vision that transcends your team and provides them with a rallying cry for where you are going.

3. They Practice Empathy

Coupled with vulnerability, Self-Evolved Leaders demonstrate deep empathy. If vulnerability is saying "here is who I am: the good, the bad, and everything else," empathy is about understanding the vulnerability of others.

We often talk about empathy as putting yourself in someone's shoes. That's a good first step, but it's much more than that. It's putting your soul (however you would describe that) in their world. It's understanding what it would be like to feel what they feel, think as they think, and act in the way they would act.

With empathy you don't get to use your perspective, your context, your faculties of reasoning. No, with true empathy all you have at your disposal to assess the situation is precisely what the person in front of you has. You think and feel and act as they would.

With empathy comes compassion, and with compassion comes a fuller picture of the impact that the decisions you make as a leader have on your team as individuals and as a group. It's the necessary foundation for helping your team develop into their best selves.

4. They Feel a Sense of Connectedness

The metaphor of each member in a team acting as a cog in a well-oiled machine is a powerful one. It brings up images of efficiency and effectiveness, of a systematic, repeatable process that can be tweaked and tinkered with and improved over time.

I'd argue, however, that it's a throwback to the industrial era of management where every input, every process, every resource could be timed, evaluated, and tweaked for performance. And when one element works too hard and starts to wear out or is deemed inefficient, it can be removed and traded for another cog of the same shape.

Instead, our teams are starting to function more like cells in organisms. The interactions are more amorphous, the nature of work is more prone to change, and the individuals are connected by more than the mere interlinking teeth of a cog or spoke. There's a stronger degree of interdependence of connection and of symbiosis. Each person is uniquely individual and at the same time part of the whole. Each person is connected by more than pursuit of a common goal; they're connected by a sense of shared humanity.

The Self-Evolved Leader recognizes this connectedness between their team members; they understand that what impacts one member impacts the others and that as a team you have the ability to positively or negatively influence not only someone's day but their career and ultimately their life.

5. They Operate from the Locus of Their Control

The final characteristic Self-Evolved Leaders demonstrate is strong ownership over what they can control and acceptance over what they can't. They understand that they can't control the external circumstances around them, whether that's politics, people, economics, or even the luck of the draw. What they can control, however, is their response to those circumstances. As such, they operate from the perspective that there are only two valid responses to a situation beyond their control: They can deal with it and find a way to make it work, or they can change their situation.

They remove any notion of a third option, so often adopted by those trapped in the Cycle of Mediocrity, which is to neither deal with the situation nor change their circumstances, but instead sit in the middle with one foot in, one foot out, complaining about it as they're swept along.

You'll find that developing these five characteristics leads to a set of external behaviors that help the Self-Evolved Leader break out of the Cycle of Mediocrity and push for excellence.

The External Behaviors of Self-Evolved Leaders

1. They Set Common Goals

Whereas the heroic leader's focus is almost exclusively on setting and achieving their own goals, the Self-Evolved Leader sets common goals for their team to rally around. More than that, though, they find a way to link the successful completion of each individual's goals to add up to the overall achievement of the team's goals.

2. They Help Their Team Achieve Those Goals

Self-Evolved Leaders understand that to achieve their personal goals, the team around them also needs to be successful. They know that if their team succeeds, they're probably ninety-five percent of the way toward achieving their personal goals. So, they dedicate most of their time to helping their team achieve their goals.

3. They Focus on the Development of Their People

While maintaining focus on helping their team achieve their individual goals, the Self-Evolved Leader doesn't actively meddle in their direct report's job. Although that may seem like a shorter route to success, they understand that at the same time as achieving their goals, their team needs to develop as individuals toward becoming the best version of themselves.

4. They Focus on the Long-Term Direction of Their Team

Self-Evolved Leaders give themselves the headspace they need to focus on the long-term direction of their team. They build appropriate rituals, routines, and firewalls to prevent themselves from getting dragged down to the day-to-day firefighting. They avoid the urge to view everything as urgent and instead spend time thinking about where the team is headed and what help it needs to get there.

5. They Move from Pull to Push

Most important of all, the Self-Evolved Leader pivots from pulling the rock up the hill while sitting above the team, to building a team that pushes it from below. This leader strives to build deep ownership and accountability in the team members and empowers them to exercise it.

What Does the Self-Evolved Leader Achieve?

If you are to do the hard work of adopting the characteristics and behaviors of the Self-Evolved Leader, not to mention developing the key elements that come after this chapter, what do you get? What is the purpose of it all? Well, the leaders I work with who make the transition typically achieve five key outcomes.

More Time and Space

Adopting the Self-Evolved Leadership approach moves you away from a constant hamster wheel of busyness to one in which you have more time and space—almost as if you're walking around in slow motion.

This time and space affords you the freedom to take a breath when making difficult decisions, allows you more room to focus on the development of your people, and helps you elevate your focus to the long-term direction of your team.

More Clarity

Self-Evolved Leaders have more headspace to make difficult decisions. When you're not juggling twenty different projects that could at any time descend into chaos, you free up some psychic RAM to analyze the situations in front of you more clearly and to make better judgment calls.

You also have a different vantage point from where to make those decisions. Rather than getting stuck dealing with the near-term distractions, you've given yourself the ability to "go to the balcony," as Harvard academic Ron Heifetz puts it. This allows you to see the whole rather than the individual parts of your team.

Better Agility

Time and clarity together give you the ability to react quickly and appropriately when you need to. Rather than making micro changes on the tactical level, you're able to see when the needs of your team change at a macro level and to react strategically.

Instead of thinking in terms of today and this week, you'll see your focus move toward this month, this quarter, and this year. That allows you to see the headwinds or opportunities that may be coming and give you time to put in place a plan to ride the wave.

High-Performing Teams

Self-Evolved Leaders produce higher-performing teams. Their dedication to helping their team develop, coupled with their ability to focus on the long term, means that they're better at spotting performance issues before they arise and working with their team members to overcome them.

They purposefully build in time to have developmental conversations with their team and strive to link the strengths of each individual to the appropriate roles and projects on their team.

Balance

Self-Evolved Leaders have more control and balance over their lives. They're able to respond appropriately and necessarily to the challenges in front of them, rather than lurching from issue to issue. They also see how the challenges they face are all a part of achieving an overarching goal or purpose that is bigger than themselves. As such, they operate with less stress and are better able to enjoy life for what it is.

The Self-Evolved Leader's Mantra

I hope, by now, you've seen the value in adopting the Self-Evolved Leadership approach. Unfortunately, this is a harder shift than it seems on the surface. Yes, it may be easy to pay lip service to the fact that you should be spending your time thinking about the strategic horizon, but in practice, it doesn't often work out like that.

The sheer number of stimuli and interruptions we receive on any given day in the workplace has a gravitational pull away from our stated goal and back toward putting out those fires.

The first thing you need to do, as with any new behavioral shift, is to adopt a new mantra, a new way of being, a new North Star that you can look to in those times of stress and pressure. If you're ready to make the first shift toward being a Self-Evolved Leader, here's the mantra you need to adopt:

"My focus is to help those on my team achieve our shared goals and, in doing so, to help them become the best version of themselves."

On the surface it seems like a simple commitment to make, almost foundational. You'd be surprised, however, at how many leaders think this is their approach but whose actions don't line up. I urge you to take this mantra and focus on it for the next six months and certainly as you read through the rest of this book. Let it guide your activities and decisions and your interactions with your team. If you do that, I can guarantee you'll have taken a massive step toward becoming a Self-Evolved Leader. The next step is to paint a renewed picture of where your team is going. You need to build a compelling vision.

WHAT TO REMEMBER

- Self-Evolved Leadership requires a shift in characteristics, behaviors, and perspective.

- Self-Evolved leaders get more time, clarity, agility, and balance.

- Your goal should be to help those on your team achieve your shared goals and, in doing so, to help them become the best version of themselves.

WHAT TO TRY

- Start each day by reciting the Self-Evolved Leader's mantra.

- Take each of the key characteristics of the Self-Evolved Leader and rate your level of ability.

- Choose one characteristic that you would like to work on and look for opportunities this week to practice that.

Go to the webpage below for a video summary of this chapter and other exclusive resources:

Selfevolvedleader.com/Chapter-2

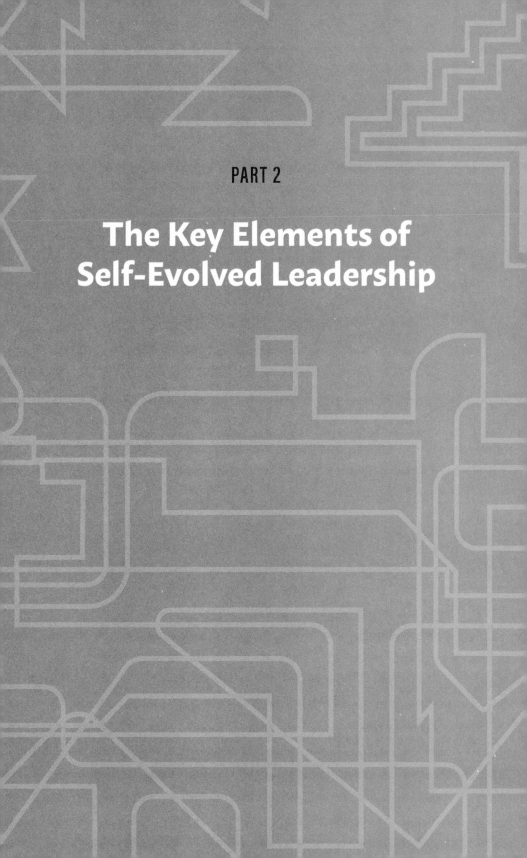

PART 2

The Key Elements of Self-Evolved Leadership

3

Vision—Set a Shared Destination

"**O**ur Vision is to build and implement a diverse range of the latest technology to deliver unique customer experiences."

I stared at the vision statement behind the receptionist's desk for a few minutes. And then I looked a little harder, hoping that it would start to make sense. I knew what each of the individual words meant and, heck, I even knew what a few of them strung together meant. No matter how much I tried, however, I couldn't quite get what it was telling me about why this company was in business.

I was sitting in the lobby of a marketing automation firm waiting for Chris, the recently appointed CEO. Chris had asked me to come in and talk to his team about vision. He had sounded pretty excited over the phone when he described the situation.

"I've got a great team, Dave," I remember him saying. "I've kept the best and brightest from the folks who were here and brought in a few of my own people who I know will help us shake this place up a bit."

"That sounds great," I replied. "So, what's the issue?"

"Well, we have a bit of an 'us and them' thing going on

between the legacy folks and the new team I brought in. They're just not seeing eye to eye."

"Ah! So, you're struggling with alignment?" I asked.

"Yeah, I guess you could put it that way. Alignment," he repeated, testing it out with himself. "So, what do we do?" he asked optimistically.

"You said you had the team together next week? Let's spend a day and unpack what's going on."

"Sounds great!" he exclaimed.

As we kick off the session, I ask the group what their collective North Star is. I'm met with blank stares, as I thought I would be.

"What's the vision for the team?" I ask. More blank stares.

"You mean the company vision statement?" someone blurts out to break the silence, then comments, "That thing has been around for years and is pretty useless."

"Yeah!" someone else chortled from the group. "That's a zinger, all right."

"OK," I said. "Let's start there."

Building a Compelling Vision

It pains me to think about the amount of time, money, and effort that have been wasted on building generic, drab, boring, uninspiring, and uninspired vision statements over the years. Not only because that time and money could have been used in much better ways elsewhere but because I've seen the power that a compelling vision statement can bring.

You see, now that you've adopted the Self-Evolved Leader's mantra from the previous chapter, you need to find a way to communicate to your team the importance of breaking the Cycle of Mediocrity and pushing toward excellence. The best place to start is in developing a new vision for your team. Here's what you get when you're able to craft a compelling vision statement.

It Builds Alignment

A good vision shows your team the possibility of the future. It presents an end state that you can collectively work toward. Presenting that common end state aligns the actions and activities that everybody takes on a day-to-day basis and points them in the same direction. As a result, you should see a stronger alignment from your team in how they communicate, collaborate, and work with each other.

It Creates a Higher Purpose

A compelling vision for your team provides them with a goal bigger than themselves to strive for. It creates a connection among your team, in that you are collectively working toward something that transcends their own capabilities.

Once considered the domain of nonprofits and social organizations, there is now an overwhelming desire from employees in all sectors to feel that the work they do contributes to a bigger goal. That the impact of what they do every day goes beyond their cubicle or the four walls of their office. There's an awakened sense of the importance of our connection to one another, to our team, to our community, and to the world.

Creating a higher purpose for your team is fast becoming one of the key distinguishing factors for attracting, hiring, and retaining top talent and a necessity for building collective morale when you go through a turbulent day, week, or month.

It Provides a North Star for Decision Making

Your team vision should be used as a guide for making decisions and a formal backstop for breaking deadlock when it occurs. One of the key characteristics of the Self-Evolved Leader is their desire to push decision making deeper into the organization. Merely granting decision-making authority at will can be problematic when there's no clear understanding of what makes a good decision. Showing your people how to use your vision statement as the arbiter for decision making can dramatically increase the strength of those decisions.

Teach your team to stop and ask the question, "Does this bring us closer to achieving our vision?" Then, encouraging them to act on it if the answer is "yes" and to put it to the side if the answer is "no" can unlock realms of decision making you didn't think possible.

Second, in those moments of deadlock where it's unclear which of two (or three) options is the best, take a step back and evaluate which path would bring you closer to achieving your vision. Then stack hands and move to implementation.

What Should It Be?

Let's be honest; most vision statements are awful! I hate to say it, but I've spent more than enough time looking at word salads of the most recent business bullcrap bingo for which a lot of time and energy were unnecessarily expended to create.

And I get it. They're hard to create. They take time and effort and wordsmithing. On top of that, we believe there's a need to sound overly professional and demonstrate your competitive advantage. The trouble is, when you go down the "vision statement generator" route, you end up with the same garbled sentiments as everyone else around you.

Rather than fall into that category, here are the characteristics of a compelling vision statement, by which you should evaluate yours.

Is It Clear?

The number one rule when building your vision statement is to be so clear that someone outside your industry, with no working knowledge of your company or its products and services, can immediately understand what it is that you're trying to achieve. Simply put, can a seventh grader understand it?

Does It Excite?

Once you've gotten past the seemingly low bar of understanding, the second test is, does it grab people's attention? Does it make those same seventh graders (or whomever else you're talking about it with) sit up and ask further questions to dig deeper and learn more?

More important, does it feel to your team that you are calling them to their own adventure? Can they see themselves contributing to it, and do they get the sense of transcendentalism that we talked about earlier? Does it make them feel that in working toward your vision, they are contributing to something greater than themselves?

Does It Present Your Why?

A compelling vision statement will explain clearly and succinctly *why* your team exists. It's less about the what or the how of what you do. Both of those are helpful to define too, but at a team level that verbiage tends to drag us down into the weeds. "We exist because . . ." is always better than "We do, or we provide . . ."

As Simon Sinek explains in his book *Start with Why*, it's much easier to buy into the "why" of an organization, a product, a team, or an individual leader than it is to buy into the what or the how. The why is what makes you unique and helps tell your team a compelling story.

Is It Connected to Your Organization's Vision?

Finally, can you show a direct link between the achievement of your team's vision and the organization's vision? For obvious reasons, unless your team has been commissioned to work in isolation or on something so new and exciting that it's completely outside the realm of anything your organization has ever attempted or achieved, there should be a through-line between the two levels of vision.

More specifically, however, this helps to provide your people with a call to an even greater purpose. The hope is that if your organization has a compelling vision, you're able to give your team an even bigger purpose to strive toward.

Second, it helps to show the value that your team provides to the organization. If there's a through-line from achieving your team's vision to the organization's vision, it's hard to argue against the necessity and appropriateness of your team.

How to Create It

There are any number of ways to build a vision statement for your team. Before we get into an approach that will produce a good outcome, here are two approaches that don't normally work. I have tried both of these myself and watched other leaders do so and struggle.

First, don't try to create a vision statement in a vacuum. As brilliant as you are, you'll likely emerge with something that is too one-dimensional to be useful and that will be hard for your team to buy into and be excited about.

On the other hand, don't try to write it by consensus. You'll end up with something that tries to appeal to too broad an audience and will likely feel insipid, watered down, or weak.

Instead, try to find a balance between both of these approaches. You need to own the process for creation and ultimately put your stake in the ground, but you also should embark on a deeply collaborative process where it is appropriate.

Here's a process that works well.

Listen, Don't Talk

The first step is to forget everything you think you know about your personal vision. Start with a blank sheet of paper and listen to your team to get a sense of what they think.

Bring your team together for a couple of hours and let them know that you want to hear their thoughts on the vision for the team. Have them discuss among themselves, then make a flip chart to present their answers to the following questions:

- What does our success look like for you?

- Why do you do what you do every day?

- If there were no barrier, what would you like to see our team achieve?

- If this was the only job you could have for the rest of your life, what would you want your legacy to be?

Getting the answers to these questions will help you ascertain from your team their understanding of what they are capable of and also give a sense of the higher goal they'd like to work toward. Both of these are vital in drafting your new team vision.

Create Coconspirators in Your Success

Once you've set the groundwork by asking the questions above, next give your team the opportunity to write a compelling vision. If you have only a small number of people working with you, then get them to do it as one group. If you have multiple people, break them into smaller groups of three to five.

Give them two hours and challenge them to come up with a vision that embodies the characteristics noted above. Then have them come back and present their findings. Widen it out to a collective discussion if you have the numbers, and ask questions to push and prod your and their understanding of what they mean. Look for common themes and linkages that arise between groups.

Doing this ensures you're considering a range of opinions when creating your vision, which prevents it from being one-dimensional. It also greatly increases the likelihood that you'll end up with something that the troops can rally behind, given their direct involvement in its creation.

Wordsmithing

By now you should have a couple of working versions of a vision statement. You'll have whatever draft versions your team pulled together plus whatever thoughts you might have. Now comes the difficult part of wordsmithing, or drafting the final version.

This is the part I don't recommend conducting in a group

setting. In doing so, you run the risk of spending a lot of time arguing over the meaning of specific words and often end up with a watered-down version of a compelling vision as you've tried to take into consideration too many varying perspectives.

Give yourself a few days to think over what you have in front of you, and then find the time to work on drafting the final version. Look for themes and patterns within the versions that your team has drafted, and continue to push for the characteristics we discussed earlier in the chapter. You're looking for something clear that excites, that presents your "why," and that is linked to your organization's vision.

Once you have something you're happy with, put it in a drawer, leave it, and completely forget about it for a week. By now you're likely too close to the vision to be able to assess its usefulness objectively. In giving yourself some space and time away from it, you allow your subconscious to chew over it, and you'll approach it with fresh eyes when you next look at it.

Feedback and Finalization

Once you return to your final draft and dust it off, it's time to get feedback on it. Go back to your team and see if it resonates with them. In general, you should be looking to see if this is something they can get behind, rather than turning this discussion into an additional round of debate on particular words or phrases.

Share it with some of your peers in the organization and your boss, and see if it reflects their understanding of your team and what you can achieve. Finally, share it with one or two people not in your organization for a sense check against the characteristics of a compelling vision. When you've collected all your feedback, make any final changes and then get it ready for release.

Sustaining Your Vision

Unfortunately, too many vision statements, even some of the good ones, die on the vine. The reason is that there's a misconception that if we put in the hard work to craft a compelling vision—one that's clear and excites and shares our why— it will automatically become self-sustaining. The reality is that once your statement is created, the hard work begins. To get a vision statement to take hold in your team, you need to spend at least six months working through the following activities.

Communicating and Stacking Hands

The first step is communicating your new vision. I suggest doing this as part of your next all-hands meeting. Be sure to thank all those involved in the process to create the vision, share with them the importance of having a good vision, and then present yours. You can bring it more to life with a story or two of why this is important to you.

Make sure to build in time for questions, and allow your team the opportunity to unpick it and understand it for themselves. At the end of the session, let the team know that having their buy-in to this vision is the only way you'll be able to get anywhere near to achieving it. Have them consider the degree to which they're willing to sign on to this as a shared vision. Even better, have them work through some form of symbolic activity to show they are stacking hands with you.

Next, you should look to build a drumbeat of communication for your new vision. Take every opportunity you can to share it with your team and those who interact with them. Only through constant repetition of your vision will it start to embed itself in your people's minds and resultant behaviors.

Perspective Shift: Toward More Vulnerable Leadership

One of the prevailing hangovers from the industrial age of leadership is the need for a leader to have absolute certainty. Certainty in direction, certainty in decision making, and certainty in results. The reality is that the world we live in is far too complex to have absolute certainty at all times. As discussed in Chapter 2, there's a strong movement toward a more vulnerable model of leadership, one that says, "I don't know the answers; here's my best guess; will you come with me on this journey of discovery?" One of the main ways a leader can explore a more vulnerable way of leadership is to give more breathing room for discussion and questions without necessarily coming to a definitive conclusion at that moment.

Sharing your new vision is a great way to practice this perspective shift. Don't fear criticism or questioning of the new vision. You may not know all the answers right now, but if you continue to work through the steps in this chapter and beyond, you'll get a little closer!

Repeat, Repeat, Repeat . . .

The second thing you need to do is to take all the communication you did in the first step above and then double it! Find every excuse to share your vision; ask your team to share it at the start of meetings, put it in your email signature, print it out on laminate cards and stick them all over your office.

This may seem like overkill to you, but in actuality, only once you feel that you couldn't possibly talk about it anymore will your people start to get it. Don't be scared of overcommunicating your vision, particularly in the first six months. It will lay a foundation that will sustain your team's success over the long run.

Team Discussion

If you're part of a wider management or leadership team, a great additional exercise is to bring together the vision statements for all the teams you lead for sharing and feedback. This can further help to sustain the vision in your team and provides new opportunities for a deeper understanding of your team's relationship with others in the organization.

Tell Stories That Celebrate Success

We tend to lean too heavily on celebrating the success that directly pertains to the day-to-day—a new deal won or a client success story. That keeps our focus on the short term. One great way to elevate that perspective and to make your vision stick is to have your team share stories where they witnessed someone embodying your vision.

Either create a stand-alone meeting to share these stories or make it a regular part of another recurring meeting. Be sure to celebrate the person in question and, where appropriate, reward their efforts.

In doing so, you'll create a culture where your team wants to go beyond achieving their day-to-day goals and to take additional steps to achieve your vision.

Make It Part of Your Onboarding Process

You know what it's like when you join a new team or new company altogether. The best-case scenario is there'll be a set of structured tasks and activities you have to work through to get yourself acclimated. At worst, you're thrown into the deep end and expected to learn to swim.

Most onboarding processes focus on the functional aspects

of doing the job, the technology you'll need, and the key people you'll be expected to interact with. Few, however, take the time to share the why of the team and what it's there to achieve. Essentially, they spend little to no time taking the new recruit through the vision.

That's a big lost opportunity. Sharing your vision with new employees early helps center them in a greater context of what they are there to achieve, prevents them having to figure out the vision through osmosis, and can be a big safety net in helping the new team member navigate through the dip in morale they will invariably hit as the realities of the role set in.

At this stage, you have adopted a new perspective on leadership and cocreated a new vision for your team. The next step is to build an implementation rhythm for delivering that vision.

WHAT TO REMEMBER

- Building a compelling vision is the first of three key elements to becoming a Self-Evolved Leader.

- A compelling vision brings alignment, a shared purpose, and a North Star for decision making.

- A compelling vision is clear, it excites, it presents your why, and it's connected to the organization's vision.

- The key to sustaining your vision is a constant drumbeat of communication.

WHAT TO TRY

- Bring your team together to explore their perspectives on your team vision.

- Have them create two or three candidates for you to wordsmith into a final statement.

- Use every opportunity to share the vision with your team, including team meetings, celebrating it in action, and as part of your onboarding plan.

Go to the webpage below for a video summary of this chapter and other exclusive resources:

Selfevolvedleader.com/Chapter-3

4

Pulse—Build an Implementation Rhythm

"It's not that we're not aligned, Dave," Chris said. "We know where we're going; we just have different ideas on how to get there."

"Almost as though you're deciding on a couple of different hiking routes to the same destination?"

"Yeah, you could say that. It's as if the sales guys want to bulldoze the forest in front of us, and the ops guys want to fashion a boat to take us down a stream." Chris chuckled.

It had been a couple of months since I'd been with Chris and his new leadership team. They had rallied around a common vision for the company, and each of the VPs had worked with their own team to create a compelling vision at that level. They had taken down the old, outdated vision statement that sat in the front lobby and replaced it with the new one, and as a group, they were relentlessly focused on communicating the new direction until they were blue in the face.

"There's a renewed sense of purpose around the place," Chris went on, trying to divert a little from the issue at hand. "You can sense it, in the hallways, in the air. It's . . . it's a new . . ."

"Energy?" I asked as Chris was fumbling for the word.

"Yeah, a new energy," he responded. "It feels as if we're on the cusp of something great."

"So where would you like to be this time next year?" I asked.

"Sitting on a beach!" Chris joked. "I'm kidding, of course. I think we can do fifty mil next year, and I'd like to see us expand our SMB offering. I think that's our real driver for growth."

"And does the team know that?"

"Oh sure, I make sure to let them know it each time I talk to them."

"But do they *really* know it? And do they know what they need to do over the next ninety days to help get closer to it?"

"I'm guessing not as much as they could," Chris said hesitantly.

"Bingo," I said. "I think it's time you and the team spent some time working on how to bring your vision to fruition."

The Importance of Building a Pulse

As we saw in the previous chapter, having a powerful, inspiring, and compelling vision for your team helps align your people around a common goal. On its own, however, it isn't sufficient for success. You'll find that there are few people for whom understanding the vantage point of where you are going is enough for them to understand how to deliver on the day-to-day.

The majority of your team will require a series of linkages that helps break that high-level vision into a series of actions. Your goal as a Self-Evolved Leader is to help provide that clarity for everyone, regardless of which vantage they feel most comfortable operating at.

The challenge, then, is to start showing the connections

between the 50,000-foot and runway levels. This involves building a set of repeatable interactions across a number of vantage points, which allows you to set and review your team's progress in a proactive rather than reactive fashion. Like the drumbeat in any piece of music, the rhythm of implementation should be steady and consistent. When you do that, you'll find your *pulse* assists in two ways.

Provides Focus for Execution

As Barry Schwartz wrote in *The Paradox of Choice*, "Learning to choose is hard. Learning to choose well is harder. And learning to choose well in a world of unlimited possibilities is harder still, perhaps too hard." Never is this truer than when working in a team with no overarching pulse. In a world where you can say yes to everything, it gets tough to focus on completing anything.

Your pulse should provide you with a set of blinkers that allows you and your team to stay ruthlessly focused for a short period. By eliminating certain choices in between review periods, you avoid the cycle of lurching from side to side in pursuit of bright, shiny new objects.

That doesn't mean you can't remain flexible and agile—quite the opposite. As you'll see below, it simply means bringing a degree of understanding and process to *how* you make that happen.

Allows for Flexibility and Agility

Too many leaders avoid building a pulse because they fear it boxes them in, that somehow it means they've become over-processed or systematized. But it's quite the opposite: A good implementation rhythm should allow you to stay agile by giving you key insight into what's working, what needs to be tweaked, and what needs to be changed altogether. In giving you a series of vantage points to review your team's progress, you're able to fit those strategic decisions to change course into the appropriate decision-making forum rather than simply walking in one day and setting fire to everything.

Five Vantage Points for Your Pulse

There are five key interactions covering a number of vantage points that you should plan with your team on an ongoing basis:

1. Annual review—50,000 feet

2. Quarterly review—30,000 feet

3. Monthly review—10,000 feet

4. Weekly review—5,000 feet

5. Daily review—runway

Let's look at them individually.

Your Annual Review
—50,000-Foot Vantage Point

Once a year, usually in the last quarter, you should bring your team together for a day to a day and a half to conduct an annual review. This review should be the key driver for all the work you and your team agree to undertake during the coming year. It's the highest vantage point you will take besides reviewing your vision and should provide one or more ambitious goals for the year ahead. There are four essential pieces to your annual review.

The Annual Stretch Goal

If you could look out one year from now and find your team has achieved one thing, what would it be? Now, if you could make that ten percent bigger, better, or faster, what would that look like?

Essentially, what would cause you to get up, high-five everybody, and then tell them they can take the rest of the day off? That's your annual stretch goal. Every annual plan should have at least one but no more than three overriding goals that drive the work you do that year.

There should be a clear link between your annual stretch goal or goals and achieving your vision. Everyone on your team should see that by achieving your overarching goals for the year, you get closer to achieving your team vision.

Quarterly Leading Indicators

Most annual stretch goals don't happen overnight; you don't suddenly go from having not achieved them to having achieved them. Along the way, you're going to pass through a couple of big milestones. Say your annual goal is to increase monthly sales to $1.5 million for two straight quarters, and your team is currently at $900,000 per quarter. You're going to have to pass through some significant numbers to get there: $1 million, $1.2 million, $1.4 million.

Or perhaps your annual stretch goal is to get average customer response time down to thirty seconds, and you're currently at fifty-five seconds. You'll have to reduce that down to sub-fifty and then sub-forty before you hit those numbers.

In both of these cases, you can track the team's performance as they work toward the annual goal. Your plan should clearly map out the intended progression to hitting those goals. In doing so, you give yourself an early indicator of whether or not you're likely to hit the target and therefore what changes you might want to make. Second, you give the team reason to celebrate smaller successes throughout the year rather than having them execute for twelve months before they get the opportunity to savor the good times.

It seems obvious, but you'd be surprised at the number of teams who don't take the time to map out their progression to achieving their annual stretch goal. When you do that, it's highly likely that enthusiasm will drain, and you'll get so fixated on the overarching goal that fear sets in and you fail to stay nimble.

Key Strategic Initiatives

By this stage, you'll have your overarching annual goal for the year and a series of quarterly leading indicators. So far, so simple? Next, you need to define your key strategic initiatives. If you know you want to reduce customer waiting time from fifty-five to thirty seconds and you have a number of leading indicators, how are you going to get there? No amount of visualization of the positive end goal is going to get you there without building some strategic initiatives.

A strategic initiative is essentially a focused project for that year explicitly designed to assist in achieving your annual goal. These can run for the whole year or just a quarter or two and can be improvements to business as usual or a brand-new project. Each person on your team should lead or be directly involved in at least one strategic initiative. Taken together, when you and your team look at the combined set of initiatives for the year, you should feel pretty confident that if you successfully run those projects, you'll achieve or come very close to your annual stretch goal.

Q1 Tactics

You could stop there, and most teams do, but I suggest you go down another level. To take your annual review down even further, and to provide a direct linkage into the 30,000-foot vantage point of execution and implementation, you should review your strategic initiatives planned for Q1 and the leading indicators you're aiming to achieve for the same period and create a list of tactics to accomplish those imperatives. At this level, you're looking for projects that you can put into action and ideally start to make progress on within the first ninety days.

Your Quarterly Review
—30,000-Foot Vantage Point

Every three months you should bring your team back together for a half day to review progress toward your annual goals. The key focus should be on deriving lessons learned from the past ninety days and agreeing on a focus for the next ninety days. The quarterly review is also the ideal opportunity to suggest and discuss possible changes or additions to your annual plan.

Review of Last Quarter

Go around the table and have each person report in on the last quarter's projects. The key questions to ask at this stage are:

- What was a success?

- What was a failure?

- What did we abandon?

- What did we learn?

- What do we need to adjust?

The discussion should be focused on gaining a collective understanding of what took place over the course of the past three months and not on aiming a firing squad at any individuals who didn't achieve their goals. Remember, your focus is on helping the team achieve their collective goals. Your initiative owners have the responsibility to deliver their plans, but you as a team have mutual accountability for supporting them to do so.

New Initiatives

Let's say you get two months into the new year, and a unique opportunity presents itself that you didn't consider during your annual planning session. It wasn't even on your radar at the time. You know, however, that if you don't move on this one, you're going to miss out, big time! What should you do? Well, first of all, slow down. The likelihood of you "missing out" on this if you don't move right now is probably lower, way lower, than you think. In fact, if it is going to be that fleeting, then chances are you're chasing a fad rather than a substantial opportunity.

Second, put the opportunity forward for discussion at your next quarterly review session. Having a data-driven debate about the pursuit of new strategic opportunities ensures that you keep everybody focused on delivering the core annual plan without yanking them from side to side or worse, throwing the whole thing in the air. Yet at the same time, it provides you with a robust mechanism to pursue new avenues.

Preview of Next Quarter

Now that you've reviewed the previous quarter and had a robust discussion about any new initiatives for the upcoming quarter, you should take the time to preview the next ninety days. Have your initiative owners give a high-level overview of the tactics they are going to implement over the next three months and any updates to their leading indicators.

Your Monthly Review—10,000 Feet

As you approach your vantage points of 10,000 feet and below, your focus should be on removing any barriers (mental or otherwise) that your team may have in order to achieve your quarterly leading indicators. While your annual and quarterly reviews give you the opportunity to live in the long-term land of the strategic, your monthly, weekly, and daily reviews should be ruthlessly focused on execution.

I suggest holding your monthly review the last week of every month. The process is pretty straightforward: Take out your leading indicators (remember, they give you the best understanding of how close you are to achieving your quarterly goals) and assign a traffic-light system to your progress:

Green—We are on track.

Yellow—There are some issues, but we could still achieve this.

Red—We are not likely to achieve this.

To keep the meeting focused on finding the shortest route to clarity, your main discussions should be around your yellow and red lights. Greens should only ever be reviewed by exception, say, if there was something extraordinary that happened that month. For any yellow lights, you should hear from your team if there is a need to put in place a recovery plan or if you should continue on your current path of execution in the belief that things will turn around.

For anything that is a red light, you should discuss any action plans that are currently in place, the likelihood of moving from red to yellow or even better to green, and what specifically you, as the leader, can do to help that.

Your Weekly Review—5,000 Feet

Your weekly review should provide you with an understanding of your team's most significant challenges for that week and how you can help them overcome those challenges. Depending on the size of your team, you should run your weekly review as a complete group, a series of one-on-ones, or a mixture of both. I suggest starting the week rather than ending it with your weekly review.

The key questions to ask are:

1. What's the most important thing you are working on this week? — What's the top priority that needs to get done for it to be a successful week for the team?

2. What's the biggest challenge you think you'll face this week? — What do they see as the potential obstacles or blockers in their way?

3. How can I best help you? — What advice, guidance, or support do they need from you in order to make this week a huge success?

Your Daily Review—Runway

Your daily review gives you an idea of what your team is working on that day and allows you the opportunity to help resolve conflicts around prioritization of work. This should be a short, sharp meeting of no more than fifteen minutes.

The key questions to ask are:

1. What did you accomplish yesterday?

2. What are your top three priorities for today?

3. What are your biggest challenges?

4. How might the team be able to help?

Making Your Pulse Work

Your implementation pulse is a powerful tool to help you and your team stay focused on the right vantage point at the right time and to collectively track your progress to achieving your goals. The realities of a complex environment and busy world mean that it's hard for all but the most disciplined leaders to maintain their rhythm. Here are some things you can do to ensure your success.

Consistency at All Costs

Your implementation pulse is about scheduling time to focus on the important aspects of your world rather than assuming you'll get there after you've dealt with everything that's urgent. The actualities of your world mean that there will be crises and emergencies that creep up all the time, presenting myriad reasons why one or more of your team may not be able to attend a meeting or why you should cancel the meeting entirely—a customer threatens to leave, you have a massive security breach, some company bigwig is coming in to town.

Having seen this happen countless times, I can tell you the urgency is almost never warranted. Instead, we talk ourselves out of these implementation meetings all the time because, let's face it, in almost every circumstance, there's something much more exciting happening elsewhere.

If you don't enforce consistency, however, you'll never break the Cycle of Mediocrity. Book your meetings for the next twelve months and enforce a rule that says attendance is mandatory in all but the most extraneous of circumstances (for you too!), and build into your communication how important this pulse is for your team as individuals and collectively.

Focus on Implementation, Not Performance

Your implementation pulse should be just that, focused on implementation. It's designed to give you and your team the best opportunity to review your progress from the necessary range of vantage points and to create the forum for agreeing on changes to your course of action when needed.

It's important not to conflate this with individual performance discussions. Sure, there may be instances when a performance issue is responsible for your team being off track, and while it's important not to avoid that issue, these meetings are not the place for having in-depth performance-related discussions. Those should be ongoing and happen in a separate forum. (Part 3 shares how to build this discipline.)

Push for Clarity in Decision Making

Getting the best outputs from each of the vantage points comes down to one thing: decision making. If your team makes and implements more good decisions than bad, you win. If you make and implement more bad decisions than good, you lose. Most teams, however, are woefully inadequate at decision making and have no cohesive process for doing so. With the emphasis on speed when it comes to decision making, most teams abdicate the process altogether. They play-act some form of discussion but end up in the position where either:

- The leader decides.

- The person with the most knowledge on the issue decides.

- The most vocal person decides.

None of these provide the foundation for a high-quality decision. They're typically too exclusive and usually offer a solution that's grounded in a win-lose philosophy of decision making.

Not only are most teams bad at making decisions, but they're also not great at deciphering the appropriate vehicle through which to make the decision. As such, decisions are either made too hastily without proper consultation, or they're squashed by never-ending debate and discussion. Here are the best ways to get to a high-quality decision-making process.

Recognize What Mode You're In

You'll likely recognize that in the vantage points outlined earlier in the chapter, there are really only three modes you and your team operate out of:

- Feedback—This is something being shared with the team for their understanding

- Decision—Something has come up, and you need to decide on it

- Assistance—Someone is requesting or offering their assistance from or to another team member

Getting good at identifying what mode you are in can significantly accelerate the effectiveness of your meetings.

Agree on the Challenge You're Trying to Solve

Once you recognize you're in decision-making mode, next, you need to clarify the specific problem you're trying to solve. Brevity is your friend here. If you can put the challenge into a one-sentence question, you'll get a much more robust discussion.

Set the Criteria for Decision Making

Before you engage in the discussion, be sure to specify how the final decision will be made: unanimous consent, a simple majority, majority plus one, a specific person in the team—these are all good options. Being clear on this will set the ground rules for your discussion, and your team can engage in the conversation appropriately.

Balance Data and Debate

At the opposite ends of every decision-making process lie data and debate. Some teams rely too heavily on data. Most rely too heavily on anecdote. To get a well-informed decision, you need to have both. Make sure that the appropriate data is gathered and circulated before the meeting and that everybody has taken the time to read it.

Second, make sure to limit the debate time to focus your discussion. Be clear that you're going to open the debate up for twenty minutes, at the end of which everybody should give their opinion on what their suggested solution is. Then default to the agreed-upon decision-making criteria from above.

Hear from Everybody

Simply put, make it a rule that everyone has to contribute at least a starting perspective to every discussion. Decisions are generally of a higher quality when a range of viewpoints are taken into consideration. Creating a safe environment for everyone to input regardless of their natural proclivity to do so can help moderate some of the more dominant voices in the room.

Have the Debate in the Room and Agreement Outside

As a team, you should be committed to having your debate and discussions in the room. Get down in the weeds, have the difficult conversations, but as soon as the decision is made, every team member should be entirely behind it even if it's not what they pushed for.

Close off the avenue to sidebar conversations and watercooler chats or even worse, calling together a subset of the team to unpick the decision. Nothing will slow down your implementation more than having one or two disgruntled members of your team.

Agree on Next Actions and a Communication Plan

Always, always, always make sure that you have complete clarity and understanding around any next actions agreed upon, who is responsible for them, and when the rest of the group will be getting an update. In addition, make sure that you have decided with whom you will communicate the outcomes of your meeting, and how that will happen. Will you send out a summary email? Do you use a shared doc service? Will it go on your team's internal comms platform?

Now that you've got your renewed team vision to show the way and your implementation pulse to manage your vantage points correctly, you need to build the disciplines necessary to execute those effectively.

WHAT TO REMEMBER

- Building an implementation pulse is a proactive way to wall off your and your team's time to focus on the important rather than get dragged into the urgent.

- Each vantage point provides its own unique perspective on the progress of your team.

- There should be a clear link between each of the interactions and achieving your overarching team vision.

- Your implementation pulse should have a ruthless focus on execution.

WHAT TO TRY

- Book in the next ninety days of your implementation pulse.

- Issue mandatory attendance, and use your walled-off time to focus on the important.

- Use a decision-making process that balances data and anecdote and provides a forum for everyone on your team to input.

Go to the webpage below for a video summary of this chapter and other exclusive resources:

Selfevolvedleader.com/Chapter-4

5

Discipline—Develop the Key Practices

"How do you think this morning went?" I asked Marco as we walked toward the refreshment table. Marco was the GM of a manufacturing company that had just recently come under new ownership, and we were working through his annual planning process.

"Pretty good!" he said with his usual bounce. "I feel as though we're getting through the agenda pretty quickly." That was precisely the problem. Unbeknownst to him, Marco was steamrolling through the agenda, leaving no real room for discussion, debate, or even a shared understanding of what we were there to achieve. As a result, anytime I asked a question, most of the team was simply deferring to his perspective.

"Do you think the folks are engaged?" I asked, hoping to lead him in the right direction.

"They're engaged enough. No less than usual," he replied. "Don't forget, they're new to some of this. So they may be a bit quieter than what you're used to."

"Of course, but I think there's something else going on." I grabbed a cup of tea and some fruit as we headed to a table. "I'm not sure if you've noticed, but every time I put something out there, you tend to share your thoughts right off the bat, and I think it's killing the conversation."

"You know me, Dave. I'm always quick to weigh in. We gotta keep moving forward."

"I get that, but I think you're building some negative behaviors in your team. I'd like to see if we can unlock some of those," I pressed.

"So, you just want me to shut up?" he said with a grin.

"No, that's not what I'm saying. At least not entirely. We need your perspective, but I'd like to give a little more space and room for the rest of the team to speak."

"And what if they don't? That'll just be awkward."

"Don't worry," I assured him. "I'm pretty comfortable with silence."

"So, what's the best way to handle this, then? You know I'm a bit of a chatter. I'm not sure I can stop doing it."

"OK, and this may sound a bit dumb. Could you literally sit on your hands?"

"Huh?" He was totally confused.

"Just try it, and every time I ask a question, equate sitting on your hands with the need to give some room for others to weigh in first."

"Seems a bit odd, but OK, let's give it a go."

The Importance of Building Leadership Disciplines

Creating a compelling vision is the most powerful way to call your team to a higher purpose and agree on a shared destination. Your implementation pulse provides you with the drumbeat to get there. Together they are a powerful duo, but on their own they are insufficient. In fact, if you were to stop there, you'd be akin to a boat captain with an engaged crew, an agreed destination, and a set of stop-off points for refueling, but who has absolutely no sea experience. When the weather changes or you go off course, you'll have no way to redirect you and your team. With all the best intentions in the world, there are three main reasons that most teams go off the map at this stage:

- The busyness of the day-to-day pulls you back to the cycle of mediocrity

- The fact you're dealing with complex individuals with their own desires and needs

- The need to operate in a larger ecosystem of your organization

The Self-Evolved Leader has the ability to foresee these elements and to build the necessary disciplines to overcome them.

What's in a Discipline?

We talk a lot about "soft skills" and "hard skills" in the workplace. Hard skills are the tangible, functional skills that you need to succeed in your role: being able to code, knowing how to use a particular piece of software, or the proficiency to drive a machine. You know those things you can point to, get certified on, and otherwise "prove" you possess.

Everything else falls under this big, mushy umbrella we like to call soft skills: communication, time management, thinking strategically, managing difficult conversations. Those are things that are a little harder to define and even more difficult to prove you possess.

The problem is that we've collectively gotten lazy in our pursuit of said soft skills. The thinking goes like this: Given they're so hard to define and prove, they must also be hard to learn and develop. Somehow, we only become better leaders through time, or maybe we read a book or go to a workshop and the lessons somehow flood our inner being, and through sheer osmosis we become a better leader. Hogwash!

When we treat leadership as a soft skill, we get soft leadership. It comes from nothing more than our collective desire to not want to put in the additional hard work to define our own development needs and to practice, truly practice our leadership.

I suggest a change in the nomenclature to help us out. Let's banish all talk of skill as it relates to leadership (soft or not) and instead start to speak in terms of disciplines. The discipline to reclaim your attention, the discipline to hold symbiotic conversations, the discipline to pause rather than act.

Disciplines are hard to master; they require an objective understanding of your relative strengths and weaknesses, and the only way to develop a discipline is through repetition and review. You try something, assess the impact, chart a new course, and try again and again and again, until it's second nature. Most important, however, disciplines are the only way to lead to ongoing, behavioral change. It's only when you've mastered the discipline that you can take the training wheels off and the behavior sticks.

The crux of becoming a Self-Evolved Leader isn't your team vision or your pulse, although they are both important. It's in mastering (or at least getting really good at) a set of interconnected leadership disciplines that help you battle against your own inner nature and that of your team and the culture of the organization around you.

In working with individuals who have made the transition to a Self-Evolved Leader, I've identified six micro disciplines and five core disciplines that they exhibit to a greater or lesser extent. We'll review the five core disciplines in Part 3 of this book. They are complex, interconnected, and can often be impacted by outside forces.

In this chapter, I'll lay out the six micro disciplines. These disciplines are more discrete, easier to master on their own, and form the basis for working through the core disciplines in the rest of the book. We'll look at each in turn and then finish with a process you can put in place to practice and review your progress. These six micro disciplines appear (or don't appear) during the interactions with your team and out into the wider organization. They can happen in a meeting, a one-on-one, a phone call, an email, or an instant message. Anywhere that you and at least one other person are interacting, you have the opportunity to practice one of these disciplines:

- Take a pause

- Exist in the present

- Set context

- Be intentional

- Listen first, talk second

- Push for clarity

To be clear, these are all learned behaviors, independent of your personality, your leadership style, your emotional palette, your thoughts or circumstances. You may be stronger in some of these and completely absent of others. However, if you put in the hard work to adopt them into your day-to-day leadership, over time you'll see the positive impact they can have.

Micro Discipline 1:
Take a Pause

In today's always connected, always on, faster-than-fast-moving world, we've eliminated any time for introspection, for reasoned decision making, and for time to think about the medium and long term. We're too busy for that. There's an actual job to be done.

In doing so, we've created a high-stress, high-reward culture for those willing to put in the hard yards and keep us moving in a direction. What we've lost is the ability to take a breath, to center our thoughts, and to give ourselves the headspace to think more innovatively and creatively.

Taking a pause can help you regain your composure in times of stress, clear your head when you need to think strategically, and create the space for collaborative solutions to emerge. It's a tool that's seldom used; it's small in stature but mighty in impact.

Your ability to let silence do the talking can unlock all manner of solutions to problems that you didn't know existed. Specifically, there are three scenarios where silence can be more profound than action.

Your Team Faces a Challenge

You're at risk of losing your biggest customer, or you've noticed a not inconsequential defect in a product that's already shipped. You're facing a problem, a crisis even, and you need a swift response. Rather than rushing to fix the problem, why not pause for a moment to make sure your response is reasoned and can be delivered swiftly?

An odd time, you may think, to take a pause. And at the macro level, you're right; you need to ensure a speedy response. To get that right, however, slowing things down at a micro level is essential. So, take a minute to gather the facts, ensure you've uncovered the root of the problem and the extent of the damage, and make sure you've identified and agreed to the key steps to fixing the problem.

You Have to Deliver Bad News

One of the least-favored parts of being a leader is delivering bad news, whether it's some critical feedback to someone on your team, pushing back on unreasonable customer demands, or perhaps even as part of your crisis management approach above. When faced with an upcoming difficult conversation, your brain kicks into a fight-or-flight response. That's why most leaders are either too combative or too meek when delivering bad news.

Rather than going in and being led by your emotions, take a moment and think through the desired outcome. Play through the conversation in your head, including the possible responses from the other side, and practice what it would feel like to give a reasoned, unemotive response to their frustrations. Pausing before delivering bad news will help center you and help you to move toward a positive outcome.

You Have a Great Idea

If you're like me, on some mornings you have at least a handful of bright ideas before you even get into the office—from new product offerings to marketing strategies, or from potential joint ventures to ways to drive down your cost base while maintaining quality. Many of those ideas likely would or at least could revolutionize your business.

Every time you unleash one of your game-changing ideas to your team, though, it sends them off into a scramble, abandoning whatever shiny new object you were pursuing last month and unclear how long this one will last before it's superseded with another.

The thing with great ideas is, if they make sense today, they'll likely still be a great idea tomorrow or next week or next month. So instead of throwing a cat among the proverbial pigeons, why not take a pause? Wait until your next quarterly review and put it out for consideration there, where your team can evaluate it next to the other strategic initiatives you are working on.

Micro Discipline 2: Exist in the Present

Multitasking is not leadership! I know you have a million and ten things to attend to, but when you're dealing with those through your computer, tablet, phone, pager, or by throwing up smoke signals rather than actively dealing with the person in front of you, you're sending them a message. You're telling them that they are not as important or at least only fractionally as important as everything else that's going on. It drains your authority; it drains your ability to be empathetic and it drains the likelihood that you will get the best outcome from the current interaction.

Building the discipline to exist in the present is a difficult thing to do in the context of a fast-moving organization, as we've developed mild addictions to the draw of something potentially more exciting. Those who master it, however, end up building stronger relationships with everyone they work with, they generate more creative solutions, and they reduce their own stress levels. Here are three things you can do to help develop this important discipline.

Turn Off Your Notifications

The ping of a new instant message or email or activity notification creates a Pavlovian response that causes us to automatically want to pick up whatever device it came from. The worst case is, we do, and we seem distracted to whomever we're talking with; or, at best, it sits at the back of our mind and eats away at us. Turn off your notifications and control how you interact with those tugs of attention.

Leave Technology Out

Even better, leave technology out of your meetings and one-on-ones completely. I know it can be helpful to take notes on a computer or tablet, but again, it's too easy to get sucked into the endless world those devices open up. Second, no one really believes all you're doing is taking notes. We all know you're checking up on other aspects. And you look less in control as a result.

Unless the technology is absolutely needed for the meeting, leave it out of the room. Take a pen and a pad of paper and focus on the conversation in front of you.

Focus on One Person or Project at a Time

When someone comes to your office with a question, focus your attention on them. When you're in a meeting, be completely in the room. When you're working on a status report, define how long you want to work on it before switching to another task, and work through it with focus. If you get interrupted, set whatever you're doing down, assess the interruption, handle it in the appropriate way, and return to what you were working on.

Micro Discipline 3:
Set Context

One of the key characteristics of a Self-Evolved Leader is their ability to maximize the outputs from their interactions. Instead of booking a one-hour meeting and letting the group fill the time, they set a clear goal and identify the time required to complete that goal. It's not that they focus on speed or efficiency at all costs, it's that they get really good at understanding how to move everyone from confusion to clarity to commitment in the shortest period of time. If that is going to take twenty minutes, good. If it requires three hours, that's equally as positive. If it can be handled over a quick email, superb!

One of the key disciplines in making that happen is to constantly set context. By that I mean helping everyone engaged in a conversation understand where in the team's pulse the conversation fits and the broader impact the decisions they come to will have. Here are the three areas to think about setting context.

The Vantage Point of the Discussion

In most interactions, participants arrive with fundamentally different perspectives on what we're there to achieve and why. The more people you have, the more likely there will be divergent perspectives. Your first goal is to quickly set the vantage point for the discussion. Is this a weekly meeting during which you're reviewing runway-level actions and need to shy away from high-level, strategic discussions? Or maybe it's a performance review, in which case it's important to stay focused on the development of your team member.

A quick context set on the vantage point can do wonders to help frame the discussion for everyone. It also gives you the foundation on which to divert particular topics as they arise that don't sit well within the current vantage point.

The Objective of the Meeting

Following quickly from setting the context of your vantage point is to agree on the objective of the interaction. Are you there to talk about a particular project, person, event, or thing? Or a mix of one or more? Setting clear expectations around what you and the people involved want to get out of your time together focuses the discussion further.

The Wider Impact of Your Decisions

Finally, as a leader in the organization, you have a unique perspective on how the discussion and decisions that you and your team are currently having will impact the wider organization. If there's a wider strategic initiative that competes with your outcome or a restructure happening that you know may make your decisions harder to implement, you should provide that context. This is not to stifle the creativity of the discussion, but more to provide some parameters to help guide the discussion.

Micro Discipline 4: Be Intentional

You'll seldom see a Self-Evolved Leader turn up for a meeting they're unsure of or chase down a rabbit hole that they know is fruitless. They are almost ruthless in their pursuit of the things that bring them closer to achieving their own and their team's goals. To practice being more intentional in your leadership, you can do three things.

Understand Your Own Goals

We spent a lot of time earlier in the book setting the collective vision for your team. Through that process, I'm sure you uncovered some things about yourself, the direction you'd like to go in, and the overarching goals you have for yourself. The starting point for being intentional in your leadership is to have an understanding of your own personal goals. This provides you with another perspective to evaluate the decisions you make on a daily basis. Spend twenty minutes or so once a quarter to review your goals and plan out how to get closer to achieving them.

Set Your Intentions

At the beginning of any major interaction, whether it's a discussion, event, project, or meeting, take two minutes and define what you want to get out of it. Ask yourself the following:

- What does success look like for you?

- How does that link to your and your team's goals?

- What roadblocks may be in your way, and how might you overcome those?

What you put into your day is directly proportional to what you get out of it. Although you can't control all the external factors, you can control your approach to them. In setting your intention, you're operating from your locus of control.

Cut Your Losses When It's Not Working

The worst thing you can do is throw more time and effort behind something that you know isn't bringing you closer to achieving your goals. The faster you can identify a dead end and back out, the better. Remember, failure in and of itself isn't a bad thing; it's how you respond to it that counts. So, if you find yourself betting on a losing approach, don't double down to try to recoup your losses; get out, reevaluate, and take another run at it.

Micro Discipline 5:
Listen First, Talk Second

This is a super simple one. As soon as you as a leader offer your opinion or perspective on a matter, the vast majority of your people are going to say, "OK, let's do that then!"

To prevent that happening, let everyone else share their perspective first. If there seems to be a consensus that isn't objectionable to you, go in that direction. If there's no consensus, share your thoughts and go around again to see if there's a common ground. If there's still no agreement, then at that point you can make the decisive call.

Give the power to your people to make the decisions they know most about, are the closest to, and will have the biggest responsibility to deliver. Allow their opinions to be heard first, and if there's silence, let it do the heavy lifting. You'll get to a stronger decision almost every time.

Although it's a simple discipline to understand, it can be very difficult for some leaders. Many have to unlearn years of bad habits of speaking before thinking and believing that their job is to know the answers. In this instance, physical reminders are your friend. These may seem a little goofy, but they're hugely effective.

Wear a Rubber Band

Put a colored rubber band around your non-watch-wearing wrist, and tell yourself that every time you see the band, it should act as a reminder to encourage your team to share before you do. In some cases, the mere sight of it can be helpful. If you need a little more help, give yourself a snap of the band every time you catch yourself talking ahead of someone else. Over time, you'll condition yourself not to do it.

Sit on Your Hands

Literally sit on your hands at your desk, in a meeting, wherever you may be. Again, you're equating a strong physical gesture with a behavior that you're trying to learn. It also helps if you sit back rather than leaning forward, as it primes your brain into thinking that you're taking a back seat in these discussions.

Use a Tchotchke to Aid Discussion

This one is a little bit *Lord of the Flies*, but it can be helpful to choreograph the conversation by using a physical object as an indicator of who has the floor to talk. Hand it out to each member of your team before you take it yourself to ensure everyone has the opportunity to contribute. This also works well in teams with members whose overeagerness to contribute can sometimes be a detriment to the quality of the conversation.

Micro Discipline 6: Push for Clarity

The last micro discipline to develop is the ability to push for clarity. Related to context setting but nuanced in its use, pushing for clarity can help keep your team aligned and in agreement when the dynamics of a discussion or decision are fluid or change over time. It's particularly helpful for difficult or substantive discussions like strategic planning or a performance-related conversation.

The Positions in the Room

In heated or tense discussions, the positions held by those involved can often be misconstrued or misunderstood, which can lend itself to straw-man arguments. There's no point having a debate or discussion around a position that isn't actually held by anyone in the room. It's an important discipline, therefore, to continually push for clarity and understanding of everyone's perspectives.

The Issue at Hand

As positions in the room change, so too do you engage in hypotheses that might not be central to the issue you're trying to solve. As much as possible, try not to get distracted by tangential discussions that may be fun to explore but which are not crucial for your purposes. Push for clarity among the group on the issue at hand, and keep conversations focused on that.

The Next Action

It's easy to emerge from a robust discussion feeling positive about the outcome and excited about the decisions that were made, only for a week to go by during which everybody involved forgot what was decided. Having a relentless pursuit of the next actions emerging from the interaction is one of the most valuable disciplines you can learn. That means pushing for engagement at a time when everyone, including yourself, is likely flagging in energy and looking to move to the next thing. Which takes us right back to the first micro discipline, take a pause.

Developing the Disciplines

Whether it's the micro disciplines in this chapter or the core disciplines in the next, the process for working on them is the same.

Conduct an Analysis

As you read through each of the disciplines, rate yourself using a traffic-light system: Green means you've got this one, yellow and you could do with a few tweaks, and red if you know you need some serious work.

Ask your team and potentially your boss to share their perspectives, and then put the micro disciplines in order from your strongest to your weakest.

Choose One or Two Things to Work On

We have a tendency to want to work on every area that we identify as a weakness at the same time. When you do that, you dilute focus and run the risk of putting in a half-hearted attempt, or worse, abandoning your development altogether. We're not very good at working on more than one thing at a time. If we were, then everybody would achieve their New Year's resolutions every year. Don't try to tackle everything all at once. Pick one or two items and definitely no more than three that you want to work on over the next ninety days.

Then map out the result you'd like to get to. Are you moving a red light to a yellow in three months or a yellow to a green? What does that look like for you? Do you want to survey the room every time you need to make a decision, or only with some groups? Do you want to pause at every piece of news, or only in particular settings? Getting clear on your goal will go a long way toward helping you achieve it.

Find an Accountability Partner

Exercisers who have a workout partner are more likely to build a discipline of going to the gym; addicts in a support group have a better chance of maintaining sobriety. As social creatures, the peer support, along with the desire to avert potential disappointment that comes with having an accountability partner, greatly increases the likelihood that we'll achieve our goals.

Working on these disciplines is no different. Find someone in your organization who you trust and know will do a good job holding you accountable to delivering what you said you would. Agree to meet with them once a month for fifteen minutes, and get into a cycle of sharing:

- What you tried since the last time you met

- What worked well

- What didn't work well

- What you're going to try between now and the next time you meet

Assess Your Opportunity to Practice

Every interaction you have with anyone in your organization on any given day gives you the opportunity to practice one or more of the disciplines. You are faced with a never-ending supply of chances to work on being more present or setting context or pushing for clarity. Rather than waste those opportunities in the busyness of the day-to-day, capitalize on one or two every week.

At first, you should choose one or two interactions that you know are happening in a given week—maybe it's your weekly team meeting, a particular one-on-one, or even a meeting with your boss—to practice your discipline. It's much easier at the beginning to plan out your approach when you know ahead of time the context of the interaction rather than trying to practice on the fly.

Over time, however, you'll notice that you're practicing your chosen disciplines randomly and at will. When you progress to this stage, you know you're moving up the ladder of mastery.

Map Your Ideal Outcome

As you review the opportunities in front of you, ask yourself what success looks like. Do you want to go into those meetings without your laptop in order to be fully present? Maybe you want to start each meeting by setting the context for your team? Whatever your end goal is, think about what that looks like, how it feels, and what the end result is for your team.

Execute

The simplest part of the whole exercise (although it may not be the easiest) is to go execute. You know what you want to work on, and you've identified your ideal outcome. Go make it happen, and don't be worried if it doesn't work out exactly how you would like it to on the first go-around. It seldom does! With each repetition, you'll get better.

Review and Repeat

Immediately following your practice session, sit down for five minutes and evaluate how it went by asking yourself the following questions:

- Did you achieve your end goal?

- If so, what worked well?

- If not, what would you do differently next time?

- What's the next opportunity you have to practice?

By repeating these seven steps over the next ninety days, you'll find that you become more comfortable in walking through the disciplines, and some may even start to become second nature to you. As a result, the interactions with your team will be stronger, more fluid, and will lead to better results. The next challenge is to take these micro disciplines and integrate them into the core disciplines in the next chapter. For that I suggest you take a moment and steel yourself. We're going to take what you've done in this chapter and turbocharge it.

WHAT TO REMEMBER

- Building leadership disciplines will help fulfill your team vision and work through your implementation pulse effectively.

- At the foundation of the five core disciplines (in Part 3) are six micro disciplines:

  » Take a pause

  » Exist in the present

  » Set context

  » Be intentional

  » Listen first, talk second

  » Push for clarity

- Working through the six micro disciplines will dramatically accelerate the impact you have on your team.

WHAT TO TRY

- Conduct a traffic-light exercise on the micro disciplines.

- Choose one or two to work on.

- Assess your opportunities to practice.

- Identify your ideal outcome.

- Execute and then review.

- Repeat!

Go to the webpage below for a video summary of this chapter and other exclusive resources:

Selfevolvedleader.com/Chapter-5

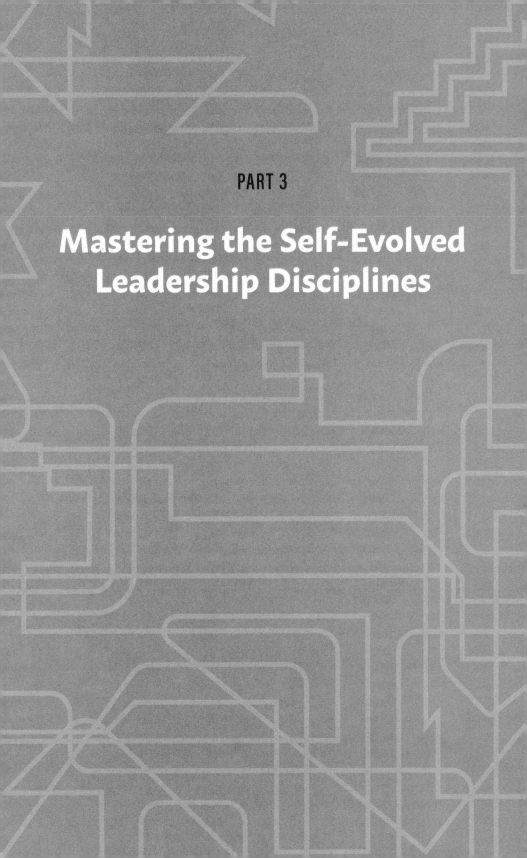

PART 3

Mastering the Self-Evolved Leadership Disciplines

6

Reclaim Your Attention

I was back sitting in Jen's office. She had been telling me how much progress she had made on moving away from heroic leadership and how she had been building her implementation pulse . . . when the behavior started.

"That's great to hear, Jen. You must be really proud of yourself—" Before I could reach the end of the sentence, she picked up her phone and started scrolling.

"Yeah!" she said, one eye on the phone and one eye on me. "I think the team's really getting a lot of value out of it too." Her words slowed to a half pace as she was clearly reading something while trying to finish the sentence.

I sat there quietly. Thirty seconds went by, and she started jabbing out a response to whatever was on the screen in front of her. Another thirty seconds went by and then she looked up.

"Sorry, what were you saying?" she said, looking back up at me with a smile.

"I wasn't; you were," I said flatly.

"Oh, yes, the team. They're getting so much out of this new process. It's great." Her phone buzzed again, and she grabbed it and starting jabbing again.

"Something you need to attend to?" I asked.

"Oh my gosh, Dave, I didn't even realize I was on my phone. How rude," she apologized.

I smiled. "Not a problem at all, Jen. We're here on your time."

"Of course." She opened her desk drawer and put the phone in. "Where should we start today?" she asked.

"How about what's got your attention," I said coyly.

Ping! The Most Important Battle in Leadership

Have you noticed that your entire life is now on interruption mode? We've basically permitted anyone to interrupt us how and when they want. Whether it's emails, phone calls, slack messages, or watercooler conversations, we're bombarded with interruptions at an incredible rate. Allowing other sources to have a hold on our attention is sapping our ability to stay present in our interactions and draining our cognitive ability to make high-quality decisions. If you want to be a Self-Evolved Leader, you have to be able to reclaim your attention.

Having a Mind Like Water

Imagine standing in front of a large, still, placid body of water. There's no tide, no wind, and it's barely moving. It's still, calm, and serene. You reach into your pocket and pull out a small pebble; smooth and round, it weighs no more than a few ounces. You take the stone and lob it into the water. Not with any great speed, you just throw it up and watch it descend. As it hits the water, a small splash and a few ripples emanate out for no more than a few seconds before the water returns to its still, steady state.

Now let's say you see a boulder at your feet. It's about the size of a baseball and weighs about four pounds. You pick it up, and with all the force and vigor you can muster, you throw it as hard as you can into the water. This time the splash is more prominent, the noise louder, and the ripples last closer to thirty seconds or so. Still, the water returns to its still, placid state.

In both these instances, the water reacts appropriately and necessary to the size, weight, and speed of each object thrown, no more, no less.

So it is with how you should respond to the interruptions in your day. Having a mind like water is taken from an old martial arts philosophy and was popularized by David Allen in his seminal book *Getting Things Done*, the premise being that you should strive to react appropriately and necessarily to those things drawing on your attention. Crises should be treated as crises and routine treated as routine. But after each tug, your mind should return to a place of placidity, ready to take the next challenge.

You know you've gotten there when you can confidently say that:

1. You can process your daily, weekly, and monthly workload with ease; and

2. Every input in your daily routine generates a necessary and appropriate reaction.

Why Is Reclaiming Your Attention Important?

I've sat in countless meetings with executive teams of varying degrees of competency in this discipline. I've seen everything, from those who pick up their phone and scroll habitually at any lull in the conversation, to those who get up loudly and declare they need to take this call because it's urgent. I've even had someone not return from a lunch break after I kindly asked her to put her phone on silent mode. In every instance, the people in the room whose focus is on what's happening in the room make better decisions, get more buy-in from their team, and get better results. Multitasking is not a leadership skill. Managing your attention to devote full focus on the task, or person, or project at hand is. Self-Evolved Leaders who get good at this, let alone master it, are able to achieve the following.

Your Focus Shifts

As you begin to get a handle on the inputs into your day and are able to manage them in the appropriate forum rather than running from crisis to crisis, you start to spend less time at runway level. Your vantage point lifts a little. All of a sudden you move from thinking about today and this week toward this month and maybe even this quarter. It won't happen all at once, but you start to feel that you have more room to think about the longer term, to be a bit more strategic.

The discussions you have with your team are more proactive, more forward thinking, and your one-on-one interactions become less remedial and more focused on growing each of the individuals on your team.

You Achieve More in a Shorter Period of Time

In *Digital Minimalism*, Cal Newport talks about "attention residue," which is a drain in momentum that occurs anytime you switch between your contexts. I'm sure you've noticed it in your own work. When you're writing a report and someone pings you on chat, it takes you a minute or two to regain your foothold when you return to your writing at the end of your conversation. Or after an interruption to a meeting, someone invariably says,

"Now, where were we?" Every time you switch between tasks, something from the interruption pulls at your psyche. In a world of few interruptions, it's no big deal. In a world where the average office worker receives literally hundreds of emails per day, that's a significant amount of attention residue slowing down your progress. And that's just one input! Think of the number of other interruptions that pull on your attention every day.

As a Self-Evolved Leader in charge of your attention, you're able to get a lot more done in a shorter period by merely minimizing this memory leakage. You become more focused and more purposeful about what you choose to dedicate your time to.

You Are More Creative

Consider the concept of the brain as a computer. In much the same way that the apps on your Mac compete for the cycles of the CPU, so too is there a competing draw in your brain. We only have limited processing power. That means that when you're trying to deal with a seemingly unlimited number of tugs on your attention, you're unable to get to the headspace to think creatively. As such, the decisions that you make tend to be the easiest, most obvious, and least likely to face opposition. By regaining control of their attention, Self-Evolved Leaders are able to free up some of their CPU cycles and generate solutions that are more creative and that ultimately have a greater impact.

You Are More in Control

Someone once told me that they visualize me on an escalator when the rest of the world is frantically running up a set of stairs. It took me a little probing to understand what they meant, but what it boiled down to was that I came across as if I was more in control of what was coming into my life (and what I was putting out) than others around me. I'm not saying I'm a master of this, not by a long way, but it is something I work hard to implement in my own life.

I'm sure you've seen someone embody a similar vibe. In a world of chaos around them, they move through it in almost slow motion, in complete control of what comes in and what goes out. As far as I see it, this happens to two groups of people: those who are pretty detached from reality and therefore unconcerned about the outcome (I'm hoping I'm not in that camp) and those who have managed to build a process for dealing with their interruptions.

Simply put, when you develop a degree of competency in this area, you feel more in control, and you seem more in control. And when you're more in control, you can manage "real" crises more effectively.

Why Is It So Hard?

We Confuse Motion with Progress

One of the overriding principles of industrial-era management is the concept of full production. This means that if some part in our system—something, someone—isn't working at full capacity, then we aren't as productive as we can be as a whole. There are instances where that absolutely holds true in today's environment: when you're cranking widgets on an assembly line, for example. In those areas where we can directly attribute the output of a person, or task, to an end result that adds value into the system, it becomes an easy equation.

The concept has spread into all aspects of our work, even in those areas where it's almost impossible to attribute output to end results. As a result, we've told ourselves that in order to demonstrate our value, we have to be "busy" and "on" at all times, otherwise we're not useful. So, we never detach from our email, we chain ourselves to our desk over lunch, and after hours, we have phone calls at the gym when we're on the treadmill. We believe that movement in a direction, any direction, is better than not, and we've blurred the lines between our work and our lives. We've confused motion with progress.

Everything Is Urgent

A key element in reclaiming your attention is becoming ruthless in your prioritization. In *The 7 Habits of Highly Effective People*, Stephen Covey popularized the "Eisenhower Matrix," a useful prioritization tool for your to-do list that has you assign a degree of urgency (how soon something needs to get done) and a degree of importance (how vital something is to get done). As a leader, the more time you can spend working on items of high importance but low urgency, the better. Things that fall into this bucket include long-term planning, developing your people, and looking for innovative ways of working. This is where you add your real value as a leader.

Unfortunately, we've allowed almost everything to fall into the high-urgency, high-importance quadrant. Every ping needs to be responded to now; every request from a customer or a boss needs to be seen to. We've allowed other people to make their crisis our emergency. As such, we spend most of our time operating in firefighting mode, running from ditch to ditch and crisis to crisis, whether or not it actually is one. We've almost entirely given up on the idea of prioritization. Either something is an emergency and it gets done now, or it's not that important and it never gets done. We spend our days forever behind the eight ball, barely keeping our heads above water, feeling as if we're moving at a million miles an hour but not ever getting anywhere.

We're Fighting an Addiction

We're all too aware of the growing addictiveness to our phones brought on by the rise of social media apps and games purposefully designed to lure our attention. Neurologists are getting stronger in their conviction that we're creating an endless cycle of seeking out pleasure from likes, shares, and retweets (triggered by dopamine) and then feeling enjoyment when it happens (triggered by the opioid system). This leads to an element of Pavlovian conditioning we're building into our relationship with technology. First, when we hear the *Ping!* or sense the vibration on our phone, the immediate reaction is to respond. Second, when we're in a period of downtime or boredom, we've trained ourselves to automatically open the news or social media or messenger apps to take us away from our tedium. Heaven forbid that we sit through a moment with nothing but our own thoughts.

If that weren't enough to keep us distracted for most of the day, I believe that our addiction to interruption has progressed a step further. In most fast-growing organizations, we've managed to get locked in the same short-term pleasure-seeking, pleasure-feeling cycle. We'd much rather respond to a short-term emergency and gain the satisfaction of solving that than dedicate time to something that may be more meaningful in the long term but that ultimately delays gratification. Now, I'm not saying that we've all turned into pleasure-seeking hedonists incapable of thinking of anything but where we'll get our next high, but we're not far off that. Think through the following questions:

- When was the last time you went longer than an hour without checking your phone?

- When was the last time you went on vacation and didn't check your email? Heck, when was the last time you went on vacation?

- When was the last time someone asked you for a quick chat or a quick meeting, and you said: "I'm afraid I can't; I'm actually working on something that I'd like to get done"?

- When was the last time you told your colleagues that you'd be unreachable for a prolonged period of time and stood by it?

In these small ways, we're training our brain to seek out something that will give us a small release of pleasure, now. We're continually searching for something that will provide us with a small reward to keep us going until the next one. As such, we gravitate toward urgency and immediacy and in turn remove our ability to do what Cal Newport calls "deep work."

How to Master Your Attention

Of all the disciplines the Self-Evolved Leader needs to develop, *attention management* stands out as number one. Failure to do so means that you'll never entirely be able to emerge from the weeds of running your team on a day-to-day tactical basis. Don't get me wrong; your team may well enjoy working with you and feel a sense of camaraderie with you, given that you're continually fighting fires with them. Unfortunately, you'll never give yourself the headspace you need to elevate your focus and take in the complete picture of your surroundings.

Here are some simple things you can do to begin to reclaim your attention.

Perspective Shift: Stop Chasing Emergencies

To start, make a perspective shift that you will stop chasing emergencies. That means two things: first, that you will not let other people's crises become your emergency, and second, that you commit to being fully present in whatever it is that you're working on in that given moment.

Get Everything Out of Your Head and Your Inbox

Your brain and your email inbox are two of the worst tools you can use as a to-do list. Your brain takes up too much energy remembering to remember, and your inbox was designed to be a communication tool. In other words, neither was designed or evolved to be used for the purpose of storing and remembering a list of things to do.

Self-Evolved Leaders practice two rituals on an almost weekly basis. First, they do a "brain dump" of everything that has their attention and put it into a paper or app-based to-do list. Second, they reduce the number of emails in their inbox to zero (or close to it) by extracting any actions and putting them into their physical to-do list and then by archiving everything else for later retrieval. Doing this frees up your brain for more complex planning, being innovative, and seeing the whole system, and it frees you up to use your email for, you know, sending email.

Become Ruthless at Prioritization

When US Airways flight 1549 struck a flock of geese about four and a half miles after taking off from New York's LaGuardia Airport and started descending rapidly, having experienced complete engine failure, Captain Chesley "Sully" Sullenberger had to act quickly. He knew this was an emergency, that what he was facing was of enormous importance and incredible urgency. At the same time, the severity of the issue became apparent to the rest of the passengers on the flight.

Sully and his first officer, Jeffrey Skiles, moved quickly but calmly through the emergency protocol they had so often trained to do, and when nothing worked, they made the tough decision to ditch in the Hudson River. Thankfully, through the skills of Captain Sullenberger and First Officer Skiles, disaster was averted and everyone was safe. Sully and Skiles did everything in their power to handle that emergency, including making the decision to ditch, which many argued was the wrong decision and further endangered the lives of all on board.

Compare that to a recent 6:45 a.m. flight out of John Wayne Airport that I was on, scheduled to fly from Southern California to Minneapolis. The time was 7:45 and we had been waiting on the tarmac for an hour on a maintenance issue when the captain came over the loudspeaker and said, "Sorry to inform you, folks, but it looks as though we're going to be another thirty minutes or so here while we try to fix this issue. I appreciate your patience." At this point, passengers started to become a little irate. Some were going to miss connections; some would miss meetings altogether. "This is ridiculous," I overheard from one passenger. Another passenger bemoaned, "They need to get it together. This is the third time this month it has happened." You see, for these passengers, this delay was not only important, but it had also now become urgent. The captain, however, knew the importance of fixing the issue, but no amount of passenger urgency was going to cause him to do anything differently than let the maintenance crew fix the problem. He wouldn't allow the passengers' crises to become the crew's emergency.

While not as dramatically, Self-Evolved Leaders take the same approach. They become ruthless at assigning a degree of importance and a degree of urgency to all they do without letting everything fall into the "crisis" category. Not only that, but they seldom allow others to define their prioritization. Like the pilot of my delayed flight, they refuse to make other people's crises their emergencies. This provides a further buffer against getting pulled into the weeds and allows them to remain calm throughout, even in a time of real emergency.

Have a Relentless Focus on the Next Action

A good friend and client of mine finishes almost every meeting with his team by asking, "What specifically would you like me to do?" After watching him do this a number of times, I asked him the reason behind it. His answer was straightforward but blew me away.

He said, "Dave, if I walk out of that meeting without clarity on the specific next action my team needs from me, then I've failed in my job."

I was intrigued, so I pushed for him to explain a bit more.

"Well, you can't action generalities. In order to get to the point of me actually doing something, my brain needs to go from their general statement and make some judgment on what action I need to take. I've learned over time that my judgment in that area usually isn't as good as I'd like it to be. Asking that question removes the guesswork for me. And them!"

Having a relentless focus on the next action for you and your team ensures complete clarity and alignment around what needs to get done and removes the noise of busyness to allow you to focus on what's important. It also reduces the natural barriers our brains throw up when we're faced with a general to-do item or project. "Q1 sales report" as a to-do is a lot harder to action than "Review Q1 sales numbers." Self-Evolved Leaders push for clarity on the next action they need to do and the next action they expect from their team.

Decide on the Right Forum for Implementation

Sometimes a day in the life of a leader feels like tennis practice. You're constantly being bombarded by furry yellow balls coming over the net and spend all day smacking them back only to be bombarded with another onslaught.

However, not all interruptions are created equal. Not all to-dos should be handled immediately; not all new thoughts need to be shared as soon as they've materialized. You shouldn't hit every interruption back over the net then and there. There is an appropriate time and place for dealing with them.

That great idea one of your team had for a new marketing plan could probably be handled at your next team meeting. The lagging sales figures for the quarter would best be addressed at your Q1 review. Your new team member who could do with a bit of guidance on their approach to the rest of the team could be coached at your next one-on-one. In Part 2 of this book, you spent some time building your pulse. One of the advantages of having done so is that you now have a number of buckets in which to put your interruptions.

Self-Evolved Leaders get really good at deciding the appropriate venue for dealing with things that come in to them on a daily basis. In filling up those other buckets, you get to keep the day in front of you as clear and free as you need.

Batch Contexts

Finally, Self-Evolved Leaders are good at batching together work that can be completed in the same setting or context and then working through a number of actions in one go. Examples of this would be scheduling a number of phone calls back to back without interruption, setting aside particular periods in the day for checking and replying to email, or stacking a couple of reports together to work through one after the other.

The reason this is helpful is due to the concept of "attention residue" that we talked about earlier. It's much easier to get into a flow of work if you can stay focused on the same type of activity for a prolonged period of time. As a result, you get more done in a shorter period of time than if you repeatedly move from one context to another.

It's even more helpful if you can match your contexts to the natural biorhythm throughout the day and week. I'm at my most productive first thing in the morning through about one p.m. on most days, so I schedule the difficult work I need to do then. I use afternoons and particularly Wednesday afternoon, which is the lowest point in my weekly productivity, for more routine or administrative tasks. Self-Evolved Leaders understand their own ebb and flow during the week as well as that of their team, and they look to maximize the peaks and be mindful of the troughs.

Team Discussion:
Toward a Common Communication Protocol

It's frustrating to watch an individual leader or manager trying their best to build a good attention-management system only to collapse under the weight of a culture of constant interruption. From being cc'd on too many emails, to needing to use a range of different communication platforms depending on the group, topic, or individual they're working with, it's easy to see how you can give up the fight.

A team can make a huge difference in its collective life by

defining a common communication protocol. Here are some things I suggest you do as a team.

1. Agree what platforms will be used for what purposes, for example, emails for formal communication, a project-management system for managing tasks and activities, and a messaging app for ongoing chats.

2. Commit to testing it out for a quarter and then reviewing. During that time, agree not to communicate via other methods unless absolutely necessary. No texts, no phone calls (unless they're part of the protocol).

3. Agree that cc'ing people on emails "for information purposes" is a waste of time. It's nothing more than either a leader's distrust in their team's ability to manage a project or a team member's desire to cover their own back. Neither of those is a good reason for doing it. If the information needs to be publicly accessible, then it's preferable to start using one of the many project-management/information-sharing systems available.

4. Make the topic of information overload an ongoing discussion, and regularly review the best way to bring speed and clarity to how you share, store, and retrieve information as a team.

Now that you've reclaimed your attention, the next step is to think about managing the flow of work in, around, and out from your team.

WHAT TO REMEMBER

· Attention management is the foundational discipline for running a successful pulse and developing the other disciplines.

· Building strong attention management is difficult, as we've given in to the addiction of busyness.

· Strong attention management will elevate your focus, allowing you to get more done in less time, be more creative, and be more in control.

WHAT TO TRY

· Once a week, get everything out of your head and email inbox and into a to-do list.

· Practice prioritization of every interruption.

· Push for clarity on the next action.

· Use specific interactions in your pulse to handle appropriate inputs.

· Batch your contexts to reduce momentum drag.

Go to the webpage below for a video summary of this chapter and other exclusive resources:

Selfevolvedleader.com/Chapter-6

7

Facilitate Team Flow

"I really wish I could get a bit more help on this," Rick said. He sounded defeated. "It's going to be a huge undertaking."

Rick was the VP of customer experience for a growing SaaS provider of data analytics for the manufacturing industry. We were sitting in his office after the senior leader's quarterly review, and it was agreed that his next ninety-day sprint needed to focus on cutting their first response times by twenty-five percent. They had seen an uptick in customer turnover, and their exit interviews indicated that response time was beginning to play a significant factor.

"I thought you said you would work with Steve on this. Remind me of his position?" I asked.

"Customer support director," Rick snapped back. "But he doesn't really have what we need for this," he continued. "He just doesn't have the rigor or follow-through. I need someone who is going to be able to look at this from all angles and come up with something that's going to work."

"And who is that?" I asked, knowing full well what the answer would be.

Rick sighed. "Well, I guess it's going to have to be me."

"Hold on, let's back up." I leaned back in my chair to try to drain some of the tension. "You're telling me that your customer support director, the person whose job it is to manage your support desk, is incapable of doing the work to reduce his team's response time by twenty-five percent?"

"Yes!" Rick exclaimed. Clearly, my efforts to remove the tension were not succeeding.

"Then why is he in that position?" I looked at Rick, dumfounded.

"OK, so maybe it's not *that* bad," Rick said with an eye roll. "He'll just need . . . a lot of hand-holding."

"And you don't want to do that?"

"No. I don't have time for that. Did you see what else came my way from that meeting? To be honest, it'll be faster if I just do it myself."

"OK," I said slowly. "And what if you have to cut your response times another twenty-five percent next quarter, or fifty? Are you going to do that yourself too?"

"Nah, I'd probably just quit," he joked.

"Seriously, though," I said. "It may take some hand-holding this time. But then you'll give Steve the chance to develop, and the next time you need something like this, he'll be able to do it with less effort on your part. In the long run, the time you invest up front will add up."

"If you say so." Rick slumped back into his chair. "But you're going to have to help me work on my intentionality because I *really* don't have time for messing around."

"Got it," I said. "Here's how I think you should approach this."

Getting Lost with Your Team

Have you ever experienced that feeling of getting lost in an activity? You become so engrossed in what you're doing that hours sometimes go by. Maybe it's practicing a musical instrument, perhaps it's writing a book, or maybe it's even getting immersed in a project at work. The Hungarian-American psychologist Mihaly Csikszentmihalyi described this as a state of "flow." When you operate in this state, you find a fine balance where the challenge of the task stretches your skills and spurs you to improve but not so much that it feels overwhelming. Flow is the middle ground between anxiety and boredom, and those who experience it regularly are usually happier, more productive, and have reduced stress levels.

Although most of the research and modern perspectives on flow have applied to the individual, the whole previous chapter, in fact, was focused on helping you achieve exactly that. Self-Evolved Leaders facilitate a sense of flow within their team.

Why Is Facilitating Team Flow Important?

The second of the core disciplines, *facilitate team flow*, is about coming to grips with the numerous inputs to your team from the wider organization or marketplace, assigning a quick prioritization, putting the most appropriate people to work on it, and then passing back the output in a smooth, efficient fashion. The goal is to give your team more authority and responsibility over the projects and tasks that come your way and to keep you focused on those areas that you can impact in the most powerful way.

Compare that with what happens daily in most teams: constant careening from side to side, regularly shifting priorities without notice, the addition and removal of tasks arbitrarily, unclear outputs and deadlines—no wonder why a team that can achieve collective flow is generally more fulfilled and productive. If you're able to build this discipline, you'll start to notice the following.

Your Team Starts to Grow

If you assume the people on your team have positive intent with the desire to learn, grow, and ultimately develop, then finding ways to give them additional projects and tasks that may be at the edge of their ability can help accelerate that process.

The additional responsibility and challenge that come from managing a task, project, or relationship that sits outside their usual day-to-day workload causes your people to learn a new talent, acquire some knowledge, or build out their own leadership disciplines. As such, this discipline gets right to the crux of the Self-Evolved Leaders' mantra: helping your people become the best version of themselves.

Facilitating team flow is one of the few routes to true empowerment. Few people enter a new team or organization with the mind-set that they have full empowerment to do whatever they want, whenever they want. Most need to feel out the boundaries of empowerment—to assess where their role begins and ends in relation to their teammates and boss, and to evaluate the resonance between what their boss says they're empowered to do and what their actions indicate is the truth.

Creating a sense of team flow makes this much clearer for both you and your teammates, and it builds a reinforcing cycle. You give responsibility and authority, they deliver, you both learn, you give a little more, they deliver again, you both learn, until eventually you take the training wheels completely off and, instead of passing over individual tasks and projects, you can delegate large portions of the work that comes into your team. Talk about true empowerment.

It Gives You More Time

In the long run, facilitating team flow will buy you back more time. It may take some up-front effort to get a system in place, but once you're able to manage that process effectively, you'll find yourself with more breathing room to think. This happens for two reasons.

The first and most obvious is that you're able to get things off your plate and, therefore, reduce your overall workload. You'll find that those things that typically sit on your to-do list for an extended period of time get shipped out quicker and come back completed more effectively.

Second, when you get really good at this, you begin to remove yourself as the bottleneck in decision making. As you strengthen the discipline, you'll find that you're delegating not only projects and tasks but aspects of decision making to the rest of your team. Over time, your team will develop a clearer understanding of the decisions you'd like them to make and will stop escalating up the chain so much or looking to you to make the final call.

It Locks In Your Elevated Focus

If your implementation pulse provides you with the set of buckets you need to proactively spend time thinking about those important, nonurgent aspects of your role, and your ability to reclaim your attention helps you manage your daily interruptions by moving them to the appropriate bucket, facilitating your team flow helps you deal with any overflow that may arise.

What you'll find, then, is that it locks in your elevated focus and prevents all but the most truly urgent from drawing you back down to the tactical runway level. That means you're able to respond more quickly to changes in the marketplace, to see ahead of time the challenges your team may face, and to concentrate on giving your team the face time that is so important for their ongoing growth and development.

Why Is It So Hard?

If we accept that facilitating team flow is an important principle, then why does it not occur more frequently, or certainly more effectively? Here are the main reasons I see for most leaders failing at this discipline.

They Misunderstand Their Value

Too many leaders believe that the value they bring to their team and organization is in their functional output rather than their ability to lead.

When you scan your team's collective to-do list with that mind-set, it becomes incredibly difficult to see opportunities to take things off your plate. Each action item is an opportunity for you to demonstrate more of your usefulness. "Compile next month's sales report"—*I'll do that*. "Create status report for next meeting"—*That's my job*.

It seems obvious. If you personally didn't do those things, what would you do? Why even have you in the position you're in? And so, you cling to those tasks as some form of security blanket.

It Takes Too Much Time

If I had a dollar for the number of times I've heard someone say, "I could give that to someone else to do, but it would be quicker for me to do it myself," I'd be dining out on that money for years. What they're effectively doing in this instance is quickly coming to the conclusion that:

Effort to show somebody *Benefit of them conducting*
how to do this task   *this task once*

This may hold true in some rare cases of unique, one-off tasks that come out of nowhere. In practice, however, the element on the right-hand side of the equation, "benefit of them conducting this task once," is usually incorrect. Realistically, you'll be showing someone on your team how to complete a task that will fall into one of the following categories.

AN ONGOING, REPEATABLE TASK

Tasks falling into this category are the easiest to spot. If something crops up repeatedly on your to-do list at regular intervals that you know someone else on your team could do with appropriate advice, guidance, and support, then it's a no-brainer to start the process. This could include things like a weekly status update, or regular changes to reports.

In this instance, the effort of you showing someone on your team how to do the task will be spread over each and every time they complete that task for the duration of their involvement with it. The equation, therefore, becomes:

Effort to show somebody *Benefit of them conducting*
how to do this task   *this task ad infinitum*

In almost every instance it's going to be worth you taking the time to work the process. Think about it: Every time they conduct said task, the effort per task is cut in half!

A TASK THAT IS INTEGRAL TO A WIDER PROJECT THEY COULD OWN

The next category of tasks you should relinquish control of are those that form part of a wider project that your team member could fully own, yet for some reason you're holding on to. I've seen many leaders seemingly delegate an entire project to someone, only to hold back on the one or two pivotal pieces on which the success of the project rests.

Almost always the retained tasks are so enmeshed in the rest of the project, and the breakdown of responsibilities is so hazy, that the leader slowly pulls back other aspects of the project at the same time as their team member cedes responsibility.

This unspoken return of delegated authority leads to frustration for both parties. The leader presumes the team member lacks ownership and accountability, while the other party believes they were never truly empowered. All of a sudden you, as the leader, are left needing to deliver the project almost in its entirety.

When at all possible, assign out projects in their entirety. That's not to say you don't need to stay informed of the project's progression, manage it from a higher level of focus, or maintain key relationships within it, but the completion of your activities shouldn't materially impact your team members' ability to complete theirs.

When you're able to assign a project in its entirety, the effort/return equation looks like this:

Effort to show somebody *how to do this task*		*Benefit of them completing* *the project*

A TASK THAT WILL INCREASE THEIR UNDERSTANDING OF THEIR ROLE

The final grouping of tasks, projects, and activities that are key candidates to give to your team are those that may help someone increase their understanding of their role. Perhaps it's something that will expand their knowledge of the products and services you sell, maybe it helps them understand one of your key internal customers better, or maybe it'll give them exposure to a more senior person who you'd like them to work more closely with.

In this instance, our equation starts to look like this:

Effort to show somebody how to do this task $<$ *Benefit of them growing in their role*

Taken together, these three scenarios leave you in a position where your busyness should never be an excuse for not entrusting your team with more responsibility and authority. The initial effort you will need to take might feel painful, but in the long run both you and your team will benefit from it.

They Don't Trust Their People

"They won't do a good enough job, and I'll have to end up fixing it anyway" is the final obstacle. Here's a glib statement. If that's one hundred percent true, then the person shouldn't be in their role. If you genuinely believe that, then it means the person is unqualified to do their job.

What leaders usually mean when they say that is, "They won't complete the task the way I would like them to," which is usually an ego-driven subjective call or an echo of our number-one excuse above, "I don't have the time to show them *how*

I would like them to complete the task." As we've just seen, that is not a good excuse.

As a Self-Evolved Leader, you should be aware enough to know not to mask ego-based judgments on the quality of someone's work nor on the excuse that you don't have time to develop someone (which are both your issues) by putting blame on the other person. It's lazy and disingenuous. Either they can't do the job, in which case you need to have a performance-related conversation with them, or you need to put in the time and effort to develop them. Don't operate in the gray area.

How to Do It

Now that you've discovered the importance of the discipline of facilitating team flow and the main reasons why most leaders don't do it, here is what you can do to ensure you manage the process effectively.

Perspective Shift: Treat Your Team as if They Will Succeed

Stop protecting people's weaknesses. Instead, treat them as if they will succeed, and be there to support and guide them as needed. That's not to say you should purposefully overburden them with a workload that they couldn't possibly handle. But if there are tasks, projects, and activities that you should legitimately be able to give to someone in their position, don't hold back because you're worried they can't do it.

Conduct a Joint Triage

I think it's safe to say that most of the people on your team aren't sitting around and waiting for work. Most of them are probably up to their eyeballs with what they need to get done today, and trying to add anything more to their plate is like pouring water into an already overflowing glass. They're not waiting for you on a Friday afternoon to pop your head into their office like Bill Lumbergh from *Office Space* to say, "I'm gonna need you to go ahead and come in tomorrow. So, if you could be here at around . . . nine, that'd be great."

Yet every time you hand over a task, project, or relationship, you're effectively doing exactly that. How, then, do you keep a ruthless focus on team flow while at the same time ensuring you don't overload your team?

The answer is to conduct joint triage. Instead of simply throwing something over the transom and hoping someone picks it up, why not start the conversation by saying, "I have something I'd like your help with; can we talk about your current workload to see if it's something you think you can fit in?" Starting the conversation this way gives your team members a sense of control over what it is you're asking them to do rather than forcing them to blindly agree to do it.

In talking through the task at hand, it's important to be explicit on the following:

- The intended outcome

- Your best guess at time and effort

- Your sense of both the urgency and importance

Getting aligned on these aspects will better serve your team in assessing their ability to get it done within the context of their wider workload.

The next question you should ask is, "Is there anything you need to move or shift around from your plate to add this in?" This provides the opportunity for your team member to negotiate their current workload, effectively saying, if you want to add that cup of water to this glass, then we need to take out another cup here. This discussion helps create a sense of joint ownership over the protection of your team members' attention and removes the feeling of isolation that sometimes comes when tasks or projects are added to their plate.

Clarity on Outcome Flexibility Elsewhere

Now that you have agreement on the context of the task at hand, next is to come to a shared understanding on the end goal and the path to get there.

Your role is to be as explicit as possible on the outcome but to be flexible with how your teammate chooses to get there. Remember, this is about providing the opportunity to learn, grow, and develop. Unless the task you're talking about is to follow a process in a specific way, give your teammate the opportunity to talk through a number of potential approaches, then provide some advice, guidance, and feedback, and ultimately support them in making the right decision.

Your Involvement and Check-In Points

Where this process can typically break down is if there's a lack of clarity between both parties on your involvement as the leader throughout the process and the key check-in points to review progress. This is a fine balance to get right: Remain too distant and detached, and you run the risk of isolating your team member and having them go too far in a slightly off-center direction. On the other hand, constant "just checking in" emails or watercooler updates can drain the trust and empowerment from the interaction.

The Self-Evolved Leader understands that their involvement should be as much or as little as their team member requires. The leader shouldn't be absent but shouldn't go looking for problems, either. Put this into practice by asking (and then listening to the answer of) some key questions.

1. HOW CAN I HELP MAKE THIS A SUCCESS FOR YOU?

You want to provide the environment for everyone on your team to succeed every time you give something to them. This question will help you understand how you might be able to create that environment, but be careful to avoid getting pulled into the trap of doing the actual work.

2. WHEN AND FOR HOW LONG SHOULD WE MEET TO REVIEW?

If you have a standing one-on-one with this person, you could suggest making your review part of your ongoing pulse. If not, or if it's an ad-hoc project, then have the person determine how often they need your eyes on it for them to succeed.

Depending on the size, urgency, and importance of the task, you may have to negotiate up or down some of their requests. As long as you can clearly articulate why you'd want to do so, then you're still leaving the control in their hands.

Asking these two questions lets your teammate know that you are available for advice, guidance, and support throughout the process but also gives you some parameters that indicate how often and in what format your interactions should be. Once you agree to those parameters, it's your job to stick with them. Be present, be available, and when needed, be helpful, but put the onus on your team to drive the conversation when they need assistance.

Review the Outcome and the Process

Once the task, project, or activity has come to a conclusion, be sure to conduct a postmortem. You want to talk through two aspects: first, how successful was the execution, and second, how well did the process work?

Let your team member lead the conversation by answering the following:

1. What worked well in both the execution and the process you followed?

2. What would you do differently next time?

3. What lessons will you both walk away with?

Doing this completes the cycle of team flow and allows you (or your teammate) to communicate back out to the wider organization or to your customers as appropriate. As you build this discipline, you'll start to notice a more consistent ebb and flow of work into, around, and back out from your team.

In an ideal world, you'd now have a system that you could set on autopilot, but in the real world you deal with complex beings who will still have their struggles and challenges. As your team works to adjust to the increase of authority, responsibility, and autonomy, questions will likely arise and roadblocks will emerge. Your ability to help them work through those issues while they still maintain control is the focus of the next core discipline: *support high performance.*

WHAT TO REMEMBER

- Aim to delegate everything except those things that only you can bring value to.

- In almost every case, time spent showing someone how to do a task or project is worth the investment.

- Effective delegation will empower your people and free up your time to spend working on their long-term areas of development.

WHAT TO TRY

- Identify all items on your to-do list that someone else on your team could do.

- Treat your team as if they can achieve what you need them to.

- Conduct a joint triage when delegating.

- Be clear on your outcome, but be flexible elsewhere.

- Have your team member identify the check-in points.

- Review your progress.

Go to the webpage below for a video summary of this chapter and other exclusive resources:

Selfevolvedleader.com/Chapter-7

8

Support High Performance

pulled up to the offices in downtown Minneapolis, excited to hear the progress Rick had made. After the last time I had met with him, he had been working hard on delegating out to Steve a pretty meaty problem they'd be working on.

I stopped to chat with the security guard for a few minutes as I waited for Rick to come down to meet me. The elevator "dinged" and he stepped out.

"Hey, Dave," he said.

I could see from his face that he wasn't in his usual cheery mood.

"Wanna go grab a coffee?" he said. "I could do with getting out of here."

"Sure!" I said. "The usual place?"

He nodded. "That would be good."

After we got our regular order, we sat across from each other, and for the next thirty minutes Rick unloaded his frustrations concerning Steve. He explained how ruthless he was in delegating out to Steve but that it seemed every five minutes Steve would be back at Rick's office with a question or query.

"So, what do you do when he turns up, looking for an answer?" I asked.

Rick paused as if I had just asked the most obvious question in the world.

"I give it to him, Dave." He stared at me blankly. "That is, after all, my job, right? Helping my team get clarity on what they need to do next."

"Sure, that's a great output." I leaned back in my chair. "But there are two ways you can go about that. You can give him the answers every time he comes knocking, or you can help him get there himself."

"Uh huh," he said, humoring me as I continued.

"And only one of those is going to stop him returning for the answers. Can you guess which one that is?" I asked with a shrug.

"Why do I have a feeling it's not the route I took?" he said with a laugh.

Moving from Managing Performance to Supporting It

Nowhere are you more prone to build learned helplessness than when someone has a problem or issue they're working through and, instead of helping them solve it for themselves, you steamroll them with a directive on precisely what they should do, or worse yet, you fix it for them. Every time you say, "Here's what you should do" or "Just leave it there, I'll deal with it," it's as if they're reaching for the button to turn off the constant racket only to discover it doesn't work. After awhile they'll stop reaching for the button.

Your goal as a Self-Evolved Leader is to be aware of this dynamic and to do everything you can to flip it on its head, to remove any chance of learned helplessness and help your people feel supported and empowered to find appropriate solutions to their challenges.

Specifically, you should move from the perspective of managing high performance to supporting it. When you try to manage high performance, you put the onus on you and your leadership skills, you remove the sense of control your people have, and you continue to push the myth that somehow you have some magic that your team doesn't possess. When you support high performance, you provide the environment from which it emerges; you push your team to assess their challenges themselves—to weigh their options and to take action. The advice and guidance you give is sparing and only used to help them unlock a difficult situation.

What Does Supporting High Performance Get You?

Following a logical thread from the previous chapter, now that you're successfully facilitating flow in your team, they're undertaking a greater number of more challenging projects and tasks. Some of these they can handle on their own, and some they'll need support with. If you adopt the approach to help support rather than manage their high performance, you'll start to notice the following.

It Creates a Stronger Relationship

Remember back, if you would, to your time at school or college, and think about your favorite teacher or professor. What was it about your teacher that still makes you feel positively about him or her? I'd be prepared to take a guess that they didn't "teach" as much as the others, that they helped you come to your own conclusions, and in turn they pulled the best work out of you. You can repeat the exercise for your favorite sports coach, or manager, mentor, leader, and dare I say it, parent or grandparent. The characteristics are all pretty similar.

We feel fondly for those in our lives who treat us as adults, give us the room to come to our own conclusions, and have a vested interest not in the end result of a particular test or game or challenge but in our long-term development.

The same applies to your team: They're looking for someone who has their back, who is truly invested in them, and who will give them the room to make their own decisions. Support them in their role and you'll build a stronger relationship with them than you would if you took a more direct managerial approach.

It Leads to Innovative Solutions

Your worldview is limited to what you've seen, read, experienced, and overcome. It's valid and it's powerful and it's what makes you uniquely you. But your worldview is a limited perspective into a world of unknowns. When you rush in with judgment or direction, you're laying that limited worldview on your team. The trouble is, they are not you and you are not them. What they've seen, read, experienced, and overcome is different from what you have.

Like the proverbial blind men describing an elephant based only on their ability to touch one portion of it, your description of the metaphorical elephant is incomplete and so is the description from any one person on your team. But in not rushing to judgment, in giving room for solutions to emerge, you create a more complete (yet never perfect) understanding of what's in front of you. As a result, your individual team members are likely to find more innovative solutions to the problems they're facing.

An Agreed Focus on Long-Term Development

Every obstacle or challenge confronting your people provides an opportunity for them to work on something longer term, to help them continue to evolve. If you've spent any time at work studying human behavior, I'm sure you'll have noticed that the issues most people have tend to group together rather than being a series of one-offs; perhaps it's a difficulty in managing relationships, or maybe they struggle to stay on top of their own attention management. We all, as humans, are pattern-driven people, whether we like to admit it or not.

Discussing obstacles or challenges with your team provides you with the opportunity to identify patterns in their behavior that may be helping or hindering their development or stunting their growth. Help them find a solution to the problem in front of them, yes, but then use that to pivot toward discussions of how they can use this situation to learn something new about themselves that they can work on over the long term.

It Provides the Opportunity to Push the Vision

Part of supporting high performance is to help your people see the problem from a number of angles and assess the options in front of them. Then, your job is to support them when they make a decision. As they work through the options in front of them, it's a good opportunity to remind them of the team vision you have. If you've effectively implemented the steps from earlier, you should be using your team vision (and ultimately your organization's vision) as your North Star for decision making. Using your supportive moments as an opportunity to remind your team of your vision can be a powerful way to help them unlock the challenges in front of them.

Why Is It Hard?

If we accept that supporting high performance is a positive thing that helps develop our people and brings more creative solutions, why, then, do we not do it more? Here are the main reasons I see for leaders not building this particular discipline.

You Have No Time!

As with many of the disciplines of the Self-Evolved Leader, the number one reason it's hard to develop them is sheer lack of time. With all the moving pieces and parts to your day job, it's hard to imagine sitting down with each person on your team and spending any length of time helping them come to a conclusion on their own. Hopefully, if you've put in place your implementation rhythm and you're working through your attention management and delegation skills, by now you'll have created the time and space needed to do this more effectively. That's one of the main reasons I suggest doing it in that order.

The Curse of Knowledge

You know the drill. Someone on your team comes to you with a problem you've seen repeatedly, or you've dealt with the exact same scenario yourself at least three or four times. You've seen what works and you know what doesn't. Given time constraints, you need to find the shortest route to an answer as quickly as possible, and so before your poor teammate can get to the end of describing their issue, you've already blurted out exactly what to do as you rush off to your next meeting. You feel pretty good, you've been helpful, and it didn't take too long, right?

Except, think about that experience from your team member's perspective. They haven't been through this issue ever before, they come looking for help to assess the problem, and before they could even finish describing it, they were sprayed with the projectile vomit of your answer. There's no learning for them, no development, only an understanding that you're the boss. The next time they're faced with an issue, they'll probably be more inclined to leave it at your door than try to fix it themselves.

The Fallacy of Certainty

The reverse side of this double-edged sword is the belief that in your position you *should* be bringing the answers. Knowing the answers and making decisions are, after all, the hallmark of your career to date. As a result, it gets so ingrained in your psyche that it starts to become an auto-response when someone turns to you. Someone has an issue; you believe that as a leader you should be sure in your thoughts. So, of course, it makes sense to help out.

Over the long haul, when you position yourself as a leader with all the answers, you create an unspoken win/loss tally running and an inherent desire to throw up more wins than losses. That's not a bad position to take in itself. Who would want to end up on a losing streak?

What happens, however, is that you start taking the safer bets, and you become less likely to push the boundaries of what is possible for you and your team. You start playing to not lose, rather than to win. Your team becomes less innovative, less comfortable with backing a riskier play, and more desirous to protect the status quo. You end up making decisions out of fear rather than hope.

Instead of operating from a place of certainty, Self-Evolved Leaders operate from a place of vulnerability, first by deeply empowering their team to make good decisions and backing them even if they fail, and second, by releasing the need for certainty. The Self-Evolved Leader takes the position that says: I have my experiences, knowledge, and skills, as do you. Each one of us has gotten to where we are through our own abilities, but our past successes shouldn't determine our future efforts. The world we operate in is too complex to rely solely on what has already occurred. No one person has all the answers; not me as the leader, not you, not our boss, not even the CEO. As a collective, however, we are much better equipped to handle what's in front of us.

How to Do It?

One of the greatest managers I've had was at a job I had early on in my career, while I was still working back in the UK. He didn't display the typical characteristics we associate with great leadership. He wasn't particularly charismatic, nor was he overly visionary, but he had an incredible way of helping groups and individuals get to the root of their problems and, therefore, solve them.

At first, I couldn't quite figure out what it was that made him so successful, so I started to observe him at every chance: with my own issues, with the issues other people would bring, and finally in a group setting.

Over time, I began to see a pattern emerge that he almost always followed. It was so natural and so seamless that I'm not even sure he was aware of it. Ever since then, I've used a similar pattern in my own coaching and training. It goes something like this:

1. Identify the root cause

2. Review the options the team has

3. Add a perspective

4. Move toward a decision

5. Provide support

The foundation of his approach throughout almost every phase was to push his team to do the hard work rather than sharing his own opinion. He provided the framework and structure for his team to come to their own conclusion, faster and with more clarity and commitment than they would have on their own, and more effectively than if this leader had told them what to do. Let's take a look at each of these stages.

Identify the Root Cause

One of the first things I noticed about how this manager dealt with these situations was how he resisted the temptation to solve the issue right away. He would spend however long it took for the person at the other end to share whatever was frustrating them at that moment.

As I'm sure you've noticed, when someone has an issue or a gripe or a challenge, they seldom clearly and succinctly spell that out for you. The real issue is usually shrouded in narrative and emotion and irrelevance. Rather than trying to make sense of that, this manager would simply wait for a pause in the monologue and then say, "OK. So, what's the issue you're trying to solve?" This subtle and obvious-seeming question would then focus their thoughts on identifying the core issue at hand that they're trying to solve. Another great question to help focus attention on the issue at hand comes from author and coaching expert Michael Bungay Stanier. In his book *The Coaching Habit*, he recommends asking "What's the real challenge here for you?" This, he asserts, helps keep your team members' attention on the issues that they specifically can impact or change rather than on those areas outside their control.

Once you have a shared understanding on the issue at hand, the next thing to help them understand is the end outcome they are looking for. Getting your team to visualize and share what success looks like does two things. First, it's a lot easier to evaluate the options in front of you when you're clear on what you're working toward. Second, it helps elevate the conversation away from the issue itself, which can often be obscured by negative emotions of frustration, anger, fear, and helplessness, and rather toward the end outcome, which is more likely to be accompanied by the positive emotions of hope, success, excitement, and happiness.

Review the Options They Have

Now that you have a shared sense of the problem they're trying to solve and a clear end goal, you move into reviewing options. The goal is to continue to push your team member for their perspective. Resist the urge to blurt out what may seem like an obvious answer to you. Instead, take a pause and ask, "What are your options?"

This again puts the onus on them to do the hard work of evaluating a course or next action. It's the starting point for empowering them to take the action they deem best suited to handle their challenge.

If they struggle with it, then begin to map out their situation. Repeat back to them the challenge they've identified and the end outcome they need to get to. Then have *them* share what they think the steps are they need to walk through to get from where they currently are, reiterating to you the challenge and the desired outcome.

It's helpful at this stage to have them review the vision of the team and organization and to ask them what options are most supportive in achieving your overall vision. Using that as a North Star in their decision-making process will greatly increase the quality of the decision they emerge with.

Add Your Perspective

You now have clarity around the challenge in front of you and what success looks like. Your team member has identified some potential solutions. Now is the time to add your perspective. As I mentioned at the top of the section, there is value in your knowledge, experiences, and skills, and they should be part of helping your team chart their path. Your goal is to provide the right balance between injecting your perspective into the conversation and creating the space for your team to solve the challenge on their own.

There are two things to consider when sharing your perspective. First, is it late enough in the conversation to not have prejudged the outcome? Second, can you share it in such a way that gets your perspective across without steamrolling the work you've already done? There's no point in going through the motions of the two steps above only to swoop in and say, "This is what you should do."

If you follow the process outlined here, you'll likely succeed in navigating the first obstacle and withhold interjecting too early in the process. Navigating the second obstacle is a little more nuanced. When adding your perspective, you should focus on helping your team evaluate the relative effectiveness of the solutions in front of them, sharing your experiences of what you've seen work well in the past, and helping them see other potential solutions in front of them that they may not have considered.

Doing this is much more valuable than flat-out saying, "I think you should or shouldn't do 'X.'" In fact, unless it's something illegal, unethical, or inappropriate, or if it's well outside the scope of their role, my suggestion is that you don't put forward your preferred course of action. That way, you give them complete freedom to make the decision for themselves.

Have Them Commit to a Plan

Now that you've helped them understand the context, reviewed their options, and shared your perspective, it's time to push them for a course of action. There's no sense in doing all that good work to end up without a clear plan.

If you've worked through the process effectively, then hopefully you should have provided the environment for your team to feel solid in their decisions. In instances where there's still a lack of clarity or hesitation, the final thing you can do is have them share what needs to happen for them to get to a point of decision. Perhaps they need more data, maybe they want to take another perspective, or maybe they need to sleep on it. All of these are good things to do if it helps unlock their choice of action.

Your job at that point is to ensure they at least have a plan of action to get to their decision point. The worst thing you can do is to send them off confused about what they want to do and confused about how they can do it.

I've Got Your Back!

The final step is to let your team know that you support them in whatever decision or course of action they decide upon, even if it's an approach you wouldn't necessarily have taken. So long as their decision is grounded in achieving the team and organizational vision, then the subjectivity surrounding how it's enacted starts to fade away.

More than just paying lip service, specifically ask your team how you may best help them execute their plan. There may be times they can handle it completely on their own, or potentially they may need a joint effort. At the very least you should offer accountability by agreeing to a check-in time.

Progress Updates and Debrief

Since you've set up your pulse from Part 2, you'll have a running agenda list for all of your direct reports. The first part of any meeting should be a review of the current tasks they've been working on. Following that should be a quick review of what's worked well since your last meeting, what didn't work so well, and what they want to achieve by the next time you meet.

Depending on the issue at hand, you may need to work through a modified version of the process above to help keep them on track. Once the challenge has been completed successfully, it's important to do a final debrief including what they've learned from the process in its entirety.

Walking through this process whenever your team faces a challenge or obstacle will likely feel a little clunky at first as you take a different tack, but over time, you'll notice that supporting your team to high performance is leaps and bounds more effective than trying to manage it.

Having said that, there are times when your conversations won't all be rainbows and butterflies. They are times when you need to have a different type of developmental conversation. That's why the next discipline focuses on having symbiotic conversations.

WHAT TO REMEMBER

- Supporting high performance rather than trying to manage it can help deepen your relationship, lead to more innovative solutions, and provide an opportunity to share your vision.

- Most leaders struggle to provide support because of an ill-placed belief in the value they add.

- Supporting high performance involves helping your team identify the root cause of the issues they face, sorting through the solutions in front of them, and then assisting them in deciding on a plan of action.

WHAT TO TRY

- The next time someone on your team has an issue, instead of solving it for them, try to help them come to their own conclusion.

- Start by identifying the root issue they're trying to solve.

- Have them share the options in front of them.

- Add your perspective.

- Push them toward action, and support the route they take.

Go to the webpage below for a video summary of this chapter and other exclusive resources:

Selfevolvedleader.com/Chapter-8

9

Have Symbiotic Conversations

"I'm reaching the end of my rope with Sarah," Chris said, his voice lifting at the end of the sentence as though he was asking a question.

"What's happened this time?" I ask. Chris was showing me around the new offices he and his team had just moved into.

"It's just her attitude, Dave. She's late to meetings, always distracted, and is the first to leave." Sarah was the VP of sales and had been at the marketing automation company before Chris took over as CEO two years ago.

"So why not have a come-to-Jesus with her? If I remember rightly, that's exactly what you said you were going to do the last time we spoke."

"She's just got so much legacy," Chris said, deflated. "She owns our biggest accounts and she knows how everything in this company happens. Also, the sales folks love her. If she walks, we run the risk of losing more than just her."

"And if she stays? What's the impact on the team?" I ask quietly.

"Well, it's already having a negative impact on everybody else.

Our leadership meetings are becoming tense as we tiptoe around the issue in the room."

"And the impact on her team?" I push a bit further.

"They see how she operates, and they follow her. They see her lack of care toward others as a badge of honor. I know most in the organization really don't like working with her, and now they're struggling to work with her team, too." He sighed and pointed to a wall of awards sitting in the lobby.

"Best place to work, five years in a row. I'm worried if we keep her around, it's going to have such a negative impact that we won't win it again this year. I just don't know what to do. And to add to it all, it's starting to make me look weak."

"So, what are your options?"

"Well, I guess I have to talk to her and hope she changes, or we're going to have to have a very different conversation."

"Would it be helpful to plan out that conversation?"

"Do a bit of role-play?" Chris joked. "I'm kidding, of course. Yes, let's do that."

The Dreaded Performance-Related Conversation

One of the key tenets of the Self-Evolved Leader is the belief and understanding that the relationships and interactions between and among their team are growing ever more connected. The impact of one team member's decisions, actions, emotions, thoughts, and behaviors have a sustained impact on the rest of the team. A great day for one can lead to an even better day for the team, a kind word can increase morale, and a toxic person can poison the culture beyond repair.

By now you've seen how the disciplines of regaining your attention, facilitating your team flow, and coaching for success,

taken together, are a mighty trio in elevating your focus and helping your team become the best version of themselves. In a perfect
world, you would be able to cycle through those three disciplines
and all would be good.

Unfortunately, we don't live in a perfect world, and things
are not that simple. No matter how good your team is or how
effective you are in leading them, at some point you will have
to have a behavioral or performance-related conversation. And
most leaders are not good at those for a number of reasons that
we'll explore. Where I've seen it work is when leaders seek to
have symbiotic conversations.

A symbiotic conversation is any interaction that acknowl-
edges the interdependence of the group and provides an opportunity for further growth among its members.

Such a conversation can be centered on a positive event, for
example, a team meeting that celebrates the individual contribu-
tions of a team member and provides the rest of the team with
the opportunity to learn from those successes. Usually, however,
and for our purposes here, the conversation is centered around a
negative event, for example, having a one-on-one discussion with
an underperforming team member.

A symbiotic conversation is one that will allow all parties
the freedom to express their reality without fear of judgment. It
seeks to find the best outcome for the team as a whole and for
the individuals within it, and it will conclude with a clear next
action that empowers people to opt in and supports those who
choose to opt out.

Let me break that down:

"A symbiotic conversation is one that will allow all parties the
freedom to express their reality without fear of judgment."

How you see a situation is different from how almost anybody else will see it. Your experience, background, knowledge,

skills, desires, what you had for breakfast this morning, the level of traffic on the road, all act as a filter on how you see the world.

Similarly, each member of your team will see things slightly differently. Allowing people the space to share how they see things and how they feel about them is a much faster way to maximize the outcome than by making assumptions.

In practice, that means giving people the floor to share how they feel without fear that their opinions will be judged or used as retribution. Once there's a shared understanding of the realities in the room, the next step kicks in:

"It seeks to find the best outcome for the team as a whole and the individuals within it."

When you approach your team from the perspective of symbiosis, you understand that each of the individuals within it has their own interests but so too does the team as a separate entity. The discussions you have seek to find the best outcome for everybody involved, including the team itself.

Thus, rather than adopting an "I win, you lose" attitude, you push for a "We win, you win, and I win" outcome. This doesn't necessarily mean pushing for the most likely or middle ground compromise. Instead it means pushing for outcomes that are outside the initial realm of thinking. It means taking time to understand everyone's desired outcomes and attempting to end up as close as possible to achieving those.

That leads to the final tenet of having a symbiotic conversation:

"It will conclude with a clear next action that empowers people to opt in and supports those who choose to opt out."

At the heart of concluding a symbiotic conversation is finding clarity on the next action. When someone is in a situation in which they're uncomfortable or unhappy, they ultimately have three choices. Either they change their situation, they stay in the current situation and complain about it, or they choose to stay in the current situation and leave their frustrations behind. In giving your team the opportunity to opt in to the next action or to opt out with support, you're essentially saying to them, "I want you to be part of this next step (staying in the current situation), but if that isn't the best outcome for you, then I fully support you in changing your situation. The one thing you're not going to do is stay in this situation and vent your frustrations. That's not in your best interests, and it's not in the team's best interests."

What Does It Get You?

Of all the disciplines for the Self-Evolved Leader to develop, having symbiotic conversations is often the hardest. Quite honestly, it feels more ambiguous than some of the others and most definitely takes more time. In a world where time is in short supply, walking through this process can feel like a less effective use of that supply.

As with the other disciplines of the Self-Evolved Leader, the time spent at the front end pays dividends in the long run. Here's what you and your team can achieve when you practice symbiotic conversations.

Elevated Morale

The discipline of having symbiotic conversations provides an atmosphere of openness, transparency, and trust. Removing the politicking that so often goes with difficult conversations and providing everyone the opportunity to share their reality turns what can so often be a negative experience into a fully positive one. If your team knows they can share their perspective without fear of repercussion and that they have the choice to opt in or out of the outcome, they'll stop operating from a place of fear and instead start to operate from a place of optimism.

A Focus on Excellence

Teams that embrace the spirit of symbiotic conversations have an elevated focus on excellence for two reasons.

Celebrating stories of success and looking for learning opportunities provide each person on your team the option to evaluate their current performance and assess if there's a next level that they want to push for or a new goal that they want to achieve. It may seem obvious, but shining a light on success is one of the fastest ways to show the stark contrast of mediocrity.

Second, when you have symbiotic conversations in a remedial fashion, say, with an underperforming employee, you're cutting off mediocrity at the knees. You're giving that individual the opportunity to opt in to the next steps to get their performance back on track, and you're further setting the tone and expectations for your team. Most leaders wait too long to have the difficult conversation, by which stage the behavior has had time to set in for the underperformer and the culture of your team has started to erode.

Clarity on Next Steps

When you engage in symbiotic conversations, you provide complete clarity on the next steps available to everyone participating. Not through some draconian ultimatum, but rather, in a way that supports the individuals involved. Even in those instances when a team member decides to opt out of the direction you're going, they have been able to come to that decision themselves and can do so with your support.

Why Is It So Hard?

Let's face it, successfully managing tough conversations is hard. They almost never go the way you want them to. Often you feel as though you've walked away without articulating your point well, and with a sense that nothing much is going to change. Here's why having those tricky interactions is difficult.

Emotional Triggers

Our brains have evolved to help us identify physically dangerous situations. Studies have shown for some time that when we feel we're in danger, our amygdala kicks in, overriding our rational thought process and causing us to either address the situation (fight) or run from it (flight). This is a positive response for helping us get out of dangerous situations quickly, but not so helpful when dealing with an upcoming conversation.

Where we haven't quite evolved is in weeding out physical threats from emotional ones. When faced with a tough interaction, the same fight-or-flight response kicks in. We literally have the same reaction as we would if we were faced with a mugger. I'm sure you've experienced it yourself. Your heart rate elevates, you can get red in the face, you start to sweat a little, and all of a sudden you find yourself stumbling over your words and getting emotional. You had a point you wanted to make, but whatever falls out of your mouth is not that. You wrap up the conversation, run back to your desk, and wonder what on earth just happened. As science writer Dan Goleman might say, "You got hijacked by your amygdala!"

We Go Either Too Strong or Too Soft

Where you naturally fall on the fight-or-flight spectrum determines a lot about your approach to those tricky conversations. If you have a tendency to go into fight mode, then you're likely to approach with guns blazing and a take-no-prisoners attitude. This almost always prevents your teammate from sensing any feel of control over the conversation, and while you may get what you want out of it, over the long run it'll damage or at least weaken your relationship.

If you usually look to avoid confrontation, then you'll do exactly that. You'll find whatever reason or excuse to not face a difficult conversation in that moment. You'll rationalize away negative behavior, tell yourself you'll wait and see how it goes, look to someone else to do the confronting, or squash the idea completely. When you take this approach, you do a disservice to the person you need to have the conversation with by not affording them the opportunity to understand the situation. Worse, still you send a message to your team that you'll tolerate underperformance or negative behavior.

"It's Not That Important"

Coupled with the point above is the belief that most performance-related issues are not that important. You hear someone make a crude joke, or they're five minutes late two days in a row. Maybe they screwed up a customer complaint and didn't report it as they should. Small things that on their own seem less important than the big picture. You think maybe it was a one-off, you want to give someone the benefit of the doubt, and you certainly don't want to nitpick.

And sure, on their own, each of those issues is not large enough for a big song and dance. Left untended to, however, they become a pattern of behavior, and your lack of willingness to address them head-on condones the behavior. So when you do need to have a discussion on someone's tardiness or inability to follow process properly, you'll be met with a blank stare that essentially says, "I've been doing this for some time now and you never had a problem, so now you're the jerk."

How Do You Do It?

Do It Often

This discipline, like any other, will improve the more you practice it. The more experience you have in overriding your amygdala and forcing your rational brain to kick in, the more you develop the muscle memory to ensure you're able to do it every time.

Given our natural proclivity to avoid difficult conversations, my advice is to have them as often as possible. I don't mean for you to invent reasons to have one, but as we saw above, we have a tendency to shy away from dealing with performance issues until they manifest themselves as a significant problem. The reality is that smaller course corrections on behavioral issues always trump big, dramatic interventions.

Commit to yourself to deal with those smaller issues when they arise. In doing so, you'll not only improve the performance of your people and the culture of your team, but you'll also improve your ability to handle these types of conversations in the future.

Assume Positive Intent

In a 2008 interview with *Fortune* magazine, Indra Nooyi, then the CEO of PepsiCo, said the greatest lesson she learned from her father was to assume positive intent. She said, "When you assume negative intent, you're angry. If you take away that anger and assume positive intent, you will be amazed. Your emotional quotient goes up because you are no longer almost random in your response. You don't get defensive. You don't scream. You are trying to understand and listen because at your basic core you are saying, 'Maybe they are saying something to me that I'm not hearing.'"

When you assume positive intent, you start from the position that the person you're talking with is a human being with the same base levels of desires and motivations as you and who, at their core, is a good person.

Assuming positive intent requires that you demonstrate vulnerability by lowering your defenses before going into a difficult situation, but it also makes you more approachable, opens up the door to collaboration or compromise, and also helps to drain some of the nervous energy you may have.

Envision a Successful Outcome and Route to Get There

You're going into a situation where a part of your brain may override your rational thought processes. The worst thing you can do, therefore, is to turn up without a clear plan or course of action.

Before any difficult conversation, envision what a successful outcome looks like. Ask yourself where you want to get to, and then map out the key points you need to make to get there. Practice empathy by thinking through how the other person may think and feel and respond, then map out your responses to those.

Close your eyes and actively see yourself in the room, having the conversation. Where do they sit; where do you sit? What hand gestures do you want to make to reinforce your points? Visualizing the conversation you're going to have will help (as much as possible) to mitigate the fight-or-flight response when it kicks in.

Feedback Is Not Criticism

Now that you've centered yourself by assuming positive intent and you've mapped out the conversation you want to have, next is to have the conversation itself. At the front end it's important to let your teammate know two overarching principles: (1) feedback is not criticism—all you're doing is giving them a chance to hear from you some feedback on their performance; (2) they retain full control over what to do with that information, and they have the choice to opt in to the next actions you'd like to see happen or to opt out and go in a different direction.

Drop Emotion and Gossip

When discussing negative behavior or a performance issue, it's easy to get caught up in emotion and narrative. Our brains make sense of the world around us by telling stories. When receiving that type of information, however, feelings and narrative are a surefire way of masking the issue at hand. It's easy to dispute stories and feelings as mere gossip or to put the blame elsewhere.

To avoid that, it's important to stick with facts and figures, with real-life examples. "You were late five times this week" is much easier to discuss than "some people on your team feel that you aren't giving the same effort." Presenting the data as data and not layering additional judgment removes the room for interpretation and argument.

State the Issue Clearly and Pause

Here's how most negative feedback goes: "I think you're doing a really good job and I enjoy working with you. However, there is one, um, thing that you might want to maybe think about working on. It's not really a big deal, but it would be good if you could have a think about it. Maybe you shouldn't [insert issue here], but as I said, totally not a big deal."

And here's what the person on the receiving end hears: "I think you're doing a really good job and I enjoy working with you and oh, I'm going to share something negative with you for the sake of it, but you can ignore that."

Nothing minimizes the authority you speak from or the severity of the issue more than dancing around the topic.

Just spit it out, clearly and concisely. And then pause. Wait for a bit longer, and then wait some more. Let the silence do the heavy lifting for you. Let the other person be the first to talk. Let them evaluate their response; don't try to force it, and don't try to anticipate it. Just let it be.

Don't Own Their Reaction

Remember that one of the key characteristics of Self-Evolved Leaders is that they operate only from their locus of control. You cannot control the reaction of anyone on your team to anything that you do. To try is futile. Yet too many leaders are scared to give negative feedback for fear of upsetting the other person. I want to be clear on this issue. Just because someone gets upset does not mean you have failed as a leader. So long as you've approached the conversation with empathy and placed control in their hands, they are the only person who can control their emotions.

Put the Next Steps in Their Hands

As you conclude the conversation, be sure to summarize your perspective and your desired next action. Let your teammate know that the choice is theirs. Either they move in the direction you agree is right for them and right for the team or they move in another direction. You will support them in whichever choice they make, but the one option that isn't available is to have one foot in and one foot out and to sit and complain.

Now that you've learned how to deal with difficult situations through symbiotic conversations, the next discipline to look at is building shared accountability.

WHAT TO REMEMBER

- Having symbiotic conversations increases team morale, helps you focus on delivering excellence, and provides clarity on the next steps.

- Most leaders struggle to have symbiotic conversations because they face a similar fight-or-flight response as to threats of physical harm.

- Having symbiotic conversations involves assuming positive intent, mapping a path to your desired outcome, and ultimately giving others the choice about what they wish to do next.

WHAT TO TRY

- Before engaging in a difficult conversation, start by assuming positive intent and mapping out what success looks like for you.

- Start the conversation by letting your team member know that feedback is not criticism and that ultimately they have a choice of how to act on the information.

- Share data and examples.

- State the issue clearly, and let the silence do the heavy lifting.

- Know that you're not responsible for their reaction.

- Put the next steps in their hands.

Go to the webpage below for a video summary of this chapter and other exclusive resources:

Selfevolvedleader.com/Chapter-9

10

Build Shared Accountability

"It just feels as though no matter what I do, they don't seem to care enough. All the all-hands meetings, the one-on-ones, the rah-rahs. I just feel as if I'm pushing this rock up a hill." Nick grabbed his beer and took two huge gulps. "On my own!" Nick was a coaching client of mine, and anytime I was in town, we'd conduct one of our coaching sessions live, in person, at a microbrewery down the road from his offices.

"So, what do you want?" I asked.

"I want them to take more frickin' responsibility, Dave. I want them to own it. I thought that by having them involved in the planning process, they'd at least feel some sense of commitment. But everyone just goes back to putting their time in."

"And what do they want, do you think?"

"A bigger paycheck, probably," Nick scoffed. "Sorry, that was a bit harsh. I don't know, I think there are some motivated people here. I just can't seem to draw it out of them."

"Well, you know, Nick. You can't teach accountability." I paused. "I mean, you can teach the principles of it. But it's up to your people whether to give it to you or not. It's their choice."

"Well, what's the point if we can't teach it to them. Why are we here?"

"Don't get antsy," I said with a smile. "You can't teach this stuff, no. But you can provide the environment in which people *want* to take ownership."

"Oh, do tell!" He perked up.

"Of course," I responded. "But it'll cost you another beer."

Building deep accountability in your team is the final piece in moving toward Self-Evolved Leadership and has been somewhat of a Holy Grail for the leadership industry over the past two decades. When your team has the desire, skills, and tools to deliver excellence as a group, with nothing more than a watchful eye from you or a few tweaks here and there, you know that you've made it.

The Importance of Building Collective Accountability

The main characteristic of a group with deep accountability is that there is enough trust, respect, and desire to see each other succeed that they're able to spur one another on toward achieving their common goals. They understand that the success of one individual is not enough on its own, particularly if the group fails. And they're able to have symbiotic conversations with each other when performance is flagging. Specifically, building collective accountability achieves the following.

Moving from Pull to Push

You know you've achieved shared accountability when the locus of decision making, direction setting, and accountability has moved away from you as the leader and into the team. You go from having the feeling that you're pulling the rock up a hill toward one where you and your team collectively are pushing it.

You notice that people take more responsibility for their work, they're comfortable taking risks, they work together to solve problems before they escalate, and the advice and guidance they seek from you is almost exclusively focused on developing over the long term.

Increased Likelihood of Achieving Your Goals

A team that has shared accountability is more likely to achieve their goals for two reasons. First, the transparency that surrounds the goal-setting process provides a psychological incentive to achieve those goals. A study by Dr. Gail Matthews, presented in 2015, highlighted that participants who shared updates on the progress of their goals regularly were seventy percent more likely to achieve them than individuals who didn't share their goals. A team that regularly updates each other on their goals, shares their successes, and drives each other on is much more likely to succeed.

Second, a focus on achieving shared goals builds a collective sense of ownership and camaraderie that can be helpful in spurring the team on. In the same way a flock of geese rotates the bird at the front to conserve energy within the group, so too can a team with shared accountability rely on each other at various times throughout their journey.

It Locks Out the Reliance on Heroic Leadership

Shared accountability is the linchpin that moves you out of the Cycle of Mediocrity and into the Cycle of Excellence. By this stage the *vision* is driving the direction of your team, your implementation *pulse* is providing you with the appropriate vantage points, and you've developed the Self-Evolved Leader's disciplines to the point where shared accountability is the natural outflow of your activities.

It's the final step in removing the need for heroics, either from you or individual members of your team. That doesn't mean there won't be challenges; of course there will: You're working with a complex, complicated group of individuals, but now there's an ecosystem built for consistency rather than frenzy.

Nor does it mean that you won't still have moments of heroism; I hope they will still happen, and they should be celebrated. When someone brings in the account you never imagined you'd get, close down early and give everyone the afternoon off. When you bust your guts to bring your customer resolution time down to under thirty minutes, take everyone out to the nicest restaurant in town. When someone discovers a rogue bug in a piece of code by staying up all night, give them a trip to Disneyland. The difference now, however, is that these acts of heroism aren't your daily operating model. They are greatness on top of excellence. They are an improvised guitar solo that takes a great song and gives it a different flavor.

Why Is It So Hard?

Wouldn't it be great if we could just jump to the bit on accountability? If, as Nick would say, we could uncover a magic bullet that gets us there? Here's the thing: No amount of teaching your people how to take ownership or be accountable will get them there. You can talk about it until you are blue in the face and they still won't get it. Here's why it's so hard to build true accountability.

Accountability Is a Choice

Deciding to take ownership and to hold yourself and others in your team accountable is an individual choice. It's up to your people to make that decision every day, and it has to come from within.

Much has been written about the power of extrinsic motivation to help shape behavior. The theory goes that, as leaders, we can manipulate performance and build accountability through either the promise of reward (a pay raise, promotion, new car) or through punishment (demotion, being frozen out, getting fired). I hope it's clear to you by now that you'll never get true accountability if you go that route. At best you'll get a group of people who can feign the behaviors of ownership for as long as the reward or threat of punishment exists.

The only place that true ownership comes from is a deep, intrinsic desire to give more effort than what's required. You can't do anything to manipulate that choice in your team. The only thing you can do is provide the environment in which your people *want* to make that choice.

Your Culture Is a Gravitational Pull

Nothing drains high performance from a group or team faster than the sense that mediocrity is being accepted and expected elsewhere in the organization. Whether that's someone higher up in the organization who is going to squash creativity and innovation and stick with the status quo no matter what you do, or another team that gets to "phone it in" on a daily basis with no repercussions, most people conform to the overriding culture of the organization they're in rather than sticking their neck out.

As a result, building pockets of accountability that sustain over the long run can be hard. While it's easy to get most groups excited about building deep ownership in the short run, if the culture of the organization is sour, that sense of ownership will only last as long as the happy hour at your next retreat.

Outdated Models and Metaphors

As with many of the transitions for the Self-Evolved Leader, it's time we progressed from an old metaphor that I believe has run its course. It's been common practice over the past decade or so to talk about accountability in terms of "owners" versus "renters."

At its core, the analogy goes something like this. Every person has the mind-set of either "owning" their job or "renting" it. Renters take the viewpoint that they'll work the role they're supposed to, do a decent enough job to avoid repercussions, and go home at the end of the day feeling OK about it. They won't, however, typically look for ways to go above and beyond their job description, nor will they try to add value to it. And, like the proverbial renter, when a problem occurs they'll call the landlord in to fix it.

Owners, on the other hand, take pride in their job, they regularly go above and beyond what's required of them, they'll seek to add value to their role, and when things go wrong, they'll fix it themselves.

We've been told to look for owners in our hiring process, reward ownership behaviors, and create an ownership culture. The analogy has proven helpful over the years, and for a long time not only have I been a proponent of it, but I've actively taught it. However, I believe it's hindering our progress, as it plays into the individualism that breeds heroic leadership.

The premise is that so long as I own *my* role, then I don't care about what anybody else does. You're another owner, awesome, I'll see you on the field. You're a renter, stay out of my way and don't bother me and it'll be OK. I'm not saying you shouldn't have a deep desire to take ownership over your individual efforts, actions, behaviors, and results—you absolutely should, it's still completely necessary. It's just no longer sufficient. Your success at all costs as an individual shouldn't outweigh our success as a team. I don't care if you score twelve goals if we let in thirteen.

Instead, we should move toward talking about collective responsibility, the belief that individual achievement is important but not at the expense of neglecting our shared goals. Unless you operate as a maverick individual contributor with limited or no interaction with another person, then your focus should be on helping the team succeed collectively.

How to Build Shared Accountability

Although you can't force your team to take accountability, there are a number of things you can do to help create the environment in which they want to.

Change Your Goal-Setting Process

The industrial-era thinking that still pervades our organizations acts to hinder personal accountability. For all the talk of transforming our performance-management processes, most organizations still roll out a version of goal setting that goes something like this: The finance team runs a model of what we achieved last year. Top leadership chooses an arbitrary percentage increase they'd like to see for the following year. More numbers are run to determine the increase in sales and output required to make that happen. Those numbers are then broken down further and cascaded through the organization until eventually, everybody has a goal. Some of the goals compete with others, most are beyond a stretch, and almost all are uninspiring.

The two main drivers for attaining the goal are either a financial incentive through a commission or an arbitrary bonus if we hit it, or the fear of a performance plan or other recourse to action if we don't hit it. We work all hours until the annual performance assessment, when we're given a thumbs-up or thumbs-down, and we all move on again to do it next year. How very Dickensian.

Instead of the old model of set and forget, your new approach to goal setting should be a collaborative, ongoing, two-way conversation. In particular, it should involve the following.

1. YOUR TEAM CREATES THEIR GOALS

Each member of your team should set their own goals rather than have them handed down. In doing so, they set a clear signal of what they believe they are capable of achieving and feel a greater drive to get there.

2. ENSURE GOALS ARE COMPLEMENTARY AND INTERDEPENDENT

Each individual and group's goals should complement one another. You should know that if one person or group succeeds, it won't be at the expense of another. There's nothing wrong with healthy competition between teams trying to achieve the same thing, but you shouldn't have two individuals who are either compensated or assessed based on mutually exclusive goals.

3. ATTACH INDIVIDUAL AND TEAM GOALS TO YOUR GOAL

In Chapter 4 we talked about setting an annual stretch goal that would establish the direction for your team over the next twelve months. Throughout the goal-setting process, you should build connections between each individual's goals and the overall goal for your team. Your message should be that each individual goal is crucial to achieving your team's goal but not sufficient. If one person achieves their goal but the group fails, then we all fail.

Your Role in Helping Your Team Set Goals

If you're putting the responsibility of goal setting on your team, what, then, is your responsibility as a leader? At a high level, you should help your people set goals that will stretch and grow them as an individual but that also aren't so ambitious to be unachievable. The best goals are ones that will help your team find a sense of flow. Here's what you should be doing.

Encourage a Growth Mind-Set

In helping your team set their own goals, you should encourage them to adopt this perspective. Carol Dweck says, "In a growth mindset, people believe that their most basic abilities can be developed through dedication and hard work—brains and talent are just the starting point. This view creates a love of learning and a resilience that is essential for great accomplishment."

Good goals, therefore, should start with the premise that their achievement will involve a development of abilities rather than one that's already within the realm of an individual's skills or talents.

When you come to review each of your team's goals, ask them how they think they will need to grow and develop in order to achieve them. If it appears that they can be achieved within the realm of their current talent and skills, push them to extend the goal or to create another tangential goal that would require further growth.

Build Deep Empowerment

The traditional goal-setting process is restricting at best and downright suffocating at worst. In particular, the binary nature of success or failure of a metric tends to lead people to create easy-to-accomplish and unimaginative goals in the first place, and second, to constrain themselves to the "usual way of doing things" to achieve them.

It can and should, however, be a liberating exercise. Encourage your team to be ambitious in their goal setting, knowing that failure is OK so long as they take it as a learning opportunity. Let them know you have their backs, and give them the freedom to achieve their goals in a manner they see fit.

Mandate Team Sharing

In order to effectively work toward a common goal and to build complementary and interrelated goals, having your team share their individual goals is a necessity. The transparency of this process deepens the level of trust in your team and their sense of connectedness. It also provides insight into what each person is motivated by and working on at any particular moment. When you do that you open up an otherwise closed box, which can bring additional sparks of collaboration and innovation between team members with shared interests or goals. At a minimum, it's best to get your team to share an update on the progress of their goals at least once a month.

Encourage Peer Accountability

Holding your team accountable for the delivery of their goals is one thing; having them hold each other accountable is entirely different. When you encourage peer accountability, it removes the sense of you as the boss checking up on their progress and strengthens a bond between peers.

Have everyone on your team buddy up, and encourage the pairs to meet with each other once a month for no more than fifteen minutes. Have each person review their successes, challenges, and lessons learned from the previous month, what they're going to work on this next month, and what, if any, help they could use from their buddy.

Tracking Progress and Providing Feedback

The collaborative nature of goal setting and accountability shouldn't take away from the fact that you can provide a useful role in helping your team achieve their goals. Your vantage point in the group will provide insight that others can't. The key mindset shift you need to make, however, is that your involvement shouldn't be a box-ticking exercise on "how things are going"; it should be an ongoing, two-way conversation to help your team members grow, develop, and achieve the goals they want to pursue. Here's how you can make that happen.

Focus on Ninety-Day Sprints

We've already seen the value in moving away from the set-and-forget process of goal setting. Instead of waiting a full calendar year before having a check-in, start to think in terms of ninety-day sprints. You should have your team break their annual goals down into quarterly chunks. At the end of every ninety days, review their progress and have them reset a goal for the next ninety-day period. This allows them to get feedback quicker on their development and to become more iterative in their approach.

Make It an Ongoing Conversation

Within those ninety days, you should keep your team members' goals front and center in your interactions and one-on-ones. This will keep you both focused on the attainment of their goals and allows you to see any areas where you may have to block and tackle for them.

Get a Dashboard

Sharing and tracking goals written on paper or buried in a series of emails is almost impossible. It's much easier if you can keep all eyes on your collective goals by creating a dashboard. It doesn't have to be anything overly sophisticated; a shared spreadsheet or Word doc would suffice. Getting everybody's goals in the same place allows you and them to keep a relentless focus on progress and gives them the opportunity to make adjustments as needed.

Pushing the Process Down

The final step in this process is to encourage your team to drive this approach down to their people. If the goal is to build an organization of genuinely empowered individuals who feel that they have the freedom to work to achieve their common goals collectively and who have a relentless focus on holding each other accountable, the only way that will truly take hold is if your team brings the concepts to their own teams.

A Final Note on Your Role

The final step you can do as a leader to help institutionalize accountability is a simple one and a defining characteristic of the Self-Evolved Leader: Give more praise than you take, and take more blame than you give. This concept may be simple in nature, but it has a massive impact on your team. Your team needs to know you have their backs. When they do, they'll start to have yours as well.

WHAT TO REMEMBER

- Building shared accountability helps you move from pulling your team uphill to working with your team to push it.

- Accountability and ownership cannot be taught; you can only provide the environment for your team to want to take it.

- Building shared accountability is a natural outflow of setting a clear vision, building an implementation pulse, and mastering the key disciplines.

WHAT TO TRY

- Have your team set their own goals.

- Link all goals to your overarching team goal.

- Encourage team sharing and peer accountability of goals.

- Focus on ninety-day sprints with your team.

- Get a shared dashboard with everyone's goals.

- Encourage your team to push the same accountability into their own teams.

Go to the webpage below for a video summary of this chapter and other exclusive resources:

Selfevolvedleader.com/Chapter-10

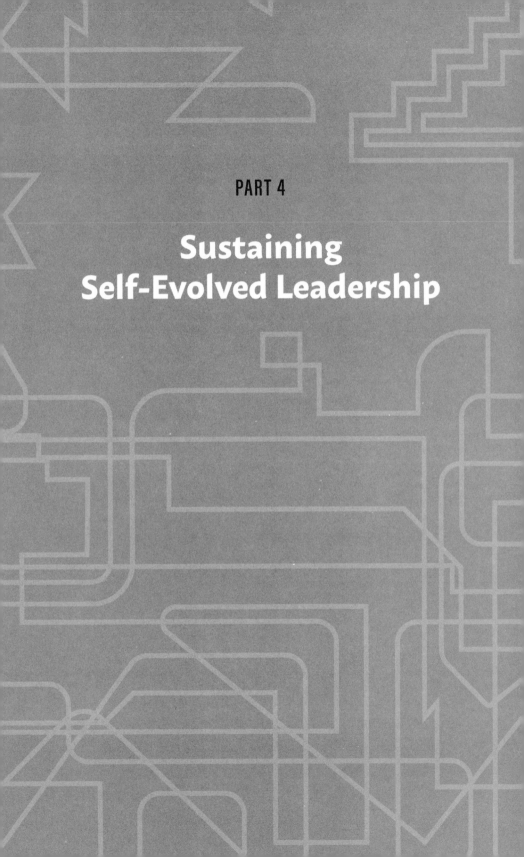

PART 4

Sustaining
Self-Evolved Leadership

11

Your Journey to Self-Evolved Leadership

O ne of the reasons we struggle to adopt new leadership philosophies or practices is that we're seldom shown how. There's a sense or belief that if we read a book, hear a talk, or go to a workshop that somehow, by osmosis, we'll absorb the information and walk away a better leader. That's akin to thinking you'll be a better basketball player by watching the NBA. When we view leadership as a soft skill, then we get soft leadership. Instead, we should view it as hard edged, something that can be practiced day in and day out. The first three parts of *The Self-Evolved Leader* provide you with the rituals, routines, and skills that you should put into practice in order to be a better leader. This final part is focused on giving you a road map for implementation.

You may have heard that it takes twenty-one days to form a new behavior. It sounds cute, but the science behind it is a little dubious. In fact, it was based on an observation by a plastic surgeon in the 1950s who noticed it took his patients *at a minimum* twenty-one days or three weeks to get used to the changes caused by the work done to their face. That has morphed over time to become the maxim that it takes twenty-one days to develop any new habit or behavior.

More recent studies have shown the number to be closer to sixty to ninety days, but the reality is that depending on the person, the task at hand, and the environment around them, this can vary even more. From my experience, behavioral changes usually take at least three months, and I almost always advocate testing out a new approach for no less than one quarter to get enough feedback on its appropriateness and efficacy.

And so, in charting your journey to becoming a Self-Evolved Leader, I suggest you start with a plan of fifteen weeks. This gives you a long enough period to implement the processes in this book at a steady pace. It ensures you're not taking on too much in one go and will prevent your newfound enthusiasm from appearing to be a fad of the month. It gives you enough time to assess what's working and what's not, and it's short enough that you won't feel you're overcommitting.

WEEK 1   Make the Perspective Shift

Your first week starts off in pure observation mode: observation of yourself, your own behaviors, and your own habits. The goal is to identify those moments when you feel you are being pulled toward heroic leadership and getting stuck in the Cycle of Mediocrity.

Key Actions

OBSERVE YOUR BEHAVIOR

As you go through the week, be mindful of your responses: to your team, to your boss, to emails, to requests, to crises, to successes, to failures. You don't need to do anything differently at this stage; simply be aware of how often your focus is dragged into the day-to-day, when you have to jump in to save the day, and when your team is relying on you for the answers. After you notice something interesting in your leadership, jot it down.

BEHAVIOR	IMPACT	LESSON LEARNED

Reflect on the Self-Evolved Leader's mantra

"My focus is to help those on my team achieve our shared goals and, in doing so, to help them become the best version of themselves."

How often do you live by this?

_____

_____

_____

How many of your interactions embody it?

_____

_____

_____

How might you better incorporate it in your day-to-day leadership?

_____

_____

_____

SET YOUR GOALS FOR THE NEXT FIFTEEN WEEKS

The path to Self-Evolved Leadership is just that, a journey and not a destination. And while the lessons in this book will help you walk that path many times, you're not likely to make a complete leap all in one goal. So, take some time at the beginning of your journey and think through what specifically you would like to achieve. Perhaps there's a particular part of the pulse you'd like to put in place, maybe you'd like to work on one or more of the disciplines, or maybe there's a relationship you'd like to impact or improve for the better? My suggestion is to jot down no more than two or three key results you'd like to achieve over the next fifteen weeks.

GOAL	HOW DO YOU KNOW YOU'VE SUCCEEDED?

Conduct a weekly review

Take ten minutes at the end of the week (I like Friday afternoons) and think through:

What worked well for you?

_____

_____

_____

What would you do differently?

_____

_____

_____

What did you learn?

_____

_____

_____

- -

WEEK 2 Create Your Vision

Week 2 focuses on the lessons in Chapter 3 on building your vision. Spend some time on individual reflection, and then record the outcomes from your planning meeting with your team.

Individual Reflection

My initial vision for the team is:

_____

_____

_____

_____

_____

Key Themes from Team Meeting

What does our success look like for you?

_____

_____

_____

Why do you do what you do every day?

_____

_____

_____

If there were no barrier, what would you like to see our team achieve?

_____

_____

_____

If this were the only job you could have for the rest of your life, what would you want your legacy to be?

_____

_____

_____

Finalize Your Vision Statement

Note down the two candidates emerging from your meeting, and then use them to finalize your statement.

VISION STATEMENT CANDIDATE 1

_____

_____

_____

_____

VISION STATEMENT CANDIDATE 2

_____

_____

_____

_____

FINAL VISION STATEMENT

_____

_____

_____

_____

- -

WEEK 3   Map Your Pulse

This week, decide on your implementation pulse. Take some time to think through the vantage points most useful to you, who should be at those meetings, and when you'd like to schedule them.

VANTAGE POINT	WHEN TO SCHEDULE THE REVIEW	WHO NEEDS TO ATTEND?
Annual review		
Quarterly review		
Monthly review		
Weekly review		
Daily review		
One-on-ones		

Implementation Pulse Agendas

Feel free to use the following agendas to guide each of your key meetings.

Annual planning

Horizon of focus: 50,000 feet
Purpose: To review the success and failure of the year before and set your focus for the next year
Timing: End of Q3
Key process:

1. Review your team's vision

2. Review last year

3. Discuss changes to your external environment

4. Review changes to the internal environment

5. Discuss candidates for your annual goal and leading indicators

6. Brainstorm strategic initiatives

7. Agree on Q1 tactics

Output: Your annual plan

Quarterly reviews

Horizon of focus: 30,000 feet
Purpose: To assess quarterly progress to annual plan
Timing: Last week of each quarter
Key process:

1. Review of last quarter

   - What was a success?

   - What was a failure?

   - What did we abandon?

   - What did we learn?

2. Review of Q1 leading indicators

   - What did we hit and why?

   - What did we not hit and why?

   - What do we need to adjust?

3. Next quarter preview

   - What should we start doing?

   - What should we stop doing?

   - What should we keep doing?

4. Share and discuss upcoming quarter leading indicators

Output: A new set of leading indicators and tactics for the next quarter

Monthly meetings

Horizon of focus: 10,000 feet

Purpose: To review leading indicators and ensure we're on track

Timing: Last week of every month

Key process:

1. Review collective dashboard

   - For green—Review only by exception

   - For yellow—Discuss if there needs to be a recovery plan

   - For red—Agree on the recovery plan

2. Agree on next actions

Output: Set of actions to help get yellow and red indicators back to green

Weekly

Horizon of focus: 5,000 feet

Purpose: To provide you with an understanding of your team's most significant challenges for that week and how you can help them overcome those challenges

Timing: Monday morning

Key process:

Ask the following questions:

1. What's the most important thing you are working on this week?—What's the top priority that needs to get done for it to be a successful week for them?

2. What's the biggest challenge you think you'll face this week?—What do they see as the potential obstacles or blockers in their way?

3. How can I best help you?—What advice, guidance, or support do they need from you in order to make this week a huge success?

Output: Agreement on your team's priorities and commitment to assist where you can

Daily huddles

Horizon of focus: Runway

Purpose: To get an idea of what your team is working on that day

Timing: First thing every morning

Key process:

Ask the following questions:

1. What did you accomplish yesterday?

2. What are your top three priorities for today?

3. What are your biggest challenges?

4. How might the team be able to help?

Output: An agreement on what everyone is working on that day

One-on-ones

Horizon of focus: Individual development
Purpose: To help your team develop the skills and behaviors to succeed
Timing: Once a week to once a month
Key process:
Ask the following questions:

1. What are your current challenges?

2. What did you try since the last time we met?

3. What worked well?

4. What didn't work?

5. What would you like to work on between now and the next time we meet?

6. How can I best support you?

WEEK 4
Assess Your Strengths and Weaknesses

Step 1: Take the Assessments

For each of the disciplines, complete the assessments below. Try to stay away from using "3" as much as possible. Calculate the average for each section.

Reclaiming your attention

	Never – Sometimes – Always				
	1	2	3	4	5
I have a clear understanding on what I need to get done today, this week, and this month.					
I systematically work through my work without stress and distraction.					
I prevent new inputs from hijacking my focus.					
When a new input arrives I quickly assign priority to it and switch focus only if needed.					
After being distracted by a new input, I return to natural flow as soon as possible.					
Average					

Facilitating team flow

Never - Sometimes - Always

	1	2	3	4	5
I delegate tasks regularly and without reservation.					
I give clear direction on the expectations of the delegated task.					
I treat employees "as if" they will meet those expectations.					
I set clear progress review opportunities.					
I allow my team members to work without undue interference between review opportunities.					
Average					

Supporting high performance

Never - Sometimes - Always

	1	2	3	4	5
I provide regular, non-performance related coaching opportunities.					
I put the onus on my team to find solutions rather than telling them what to do.					
I ask non-leading questions to help my team assess their options.					
I trust my team to make the right decisions.					
I provide a non-judgmental environment for my team to review their success.					
Average					

Having symbiotic conversations

Never – Sometimes – Always

	1	2	3	4	5
I engage in (rather than avoid) difficult conversations when necessary.					
I attempt to uncover the issue at hand rather than engaging in gossip.					
I stay focused on data & examples rather than narrative & anecdote.					
I ensure participants in the conversation feel heard.					
I seek an outcome that's in the best interest of all participants.					
Average					

Building shared accountability

Never – Sometimes – Always

	1	2	3	4	5
I hold myself accountable to deliver on my commitments.					
I take responsibility when I individually, or we as a team, fail.					
I provide appropriate remedies for failure.					
I hold my team accountable to deliver on their commitments.					
I provide praise and acknowledgment when we succeed as a team.					
Average					

STEP 2: Rank Your Disciplines

Using the average score for each section, rank your skills from strongest to weakest.

DISCIPLINE	SCORE
_____	_____
_____	_____
_____	_____
_____	_____
_____	_____
_____	_____

STEP 3: Rank Your Individual Behaviors

Look across all the individual questions and gather your five strongest behaviors and five weakest.

STRONGEST BEHAVIORS	SCORE
_____	_____
_____	_____
_____	_____
_____	_____
_____	_____

WEAKEST BEHAVIORS	SCORE
_____	_____
_____	_____
_____	_____
_____	_____
_____	_____

WEEK 5 Build Your Mastery Plan

Taking the assessments from the previous section and any other inputs you'd like, map out one to three key areas to work on over the next ten weeks.

AREA 1

What do you want to work on (behavior, discipline, mind-set shift)?

_____

_____

_____

What specifically do you want to achieve?

_____

_____

_____

How will you know you've succeeded?

_____

_____

_____

What resources can you access to help in this area? (books, webinars, programs, etc.)

_____

_____

_____

What opportunities do you have on the job to work on this?

_____

_____

_____

Who in your organization is really good at this?

_____

_____

_____

Who will you ask to hold you accountable?

_____

_____

_____

What's your next action to make progress?

_____

_____

_____

What's your next date to review?

_____

_____

_____

AREA 2

What do you want to work on (behavior, discipline, mind-set shift)?

_____

_____

_____

What specifically do you want to achieve?

_____

_____

_____

How will you know you've succeeded?

_____

_____

_____

What resources can you access to help in this area? (books, webinars, programs, etc.)

_____

_____

_____

What opportunities do you have on the job to work on this?

_____

_____

_____

Who in your organization is really good at this?

_____

_____

_____

Who will you ask to hold you accountable?

_____

_____

_____

What's your next action to make progress?

_____

_____

_____

What's your next date to review?

_____

_____

_____

AREA 3

What do you want to work on (behavior, discipline, mind-set shift)?

_____

_____

_____

What specifically do you want to achieve?

_____

_____

_____

How will you know you've succeeded?

_____

_____

_____

What resources can you access to help in this area? (books, webinars, programs, etc.)

_____

_____

_____

What opportunities do you have on the job to work on this?

_____

_____

_____

Who in your organization is really good at this?

_____

_____

_____

Who will you ask to hold you accountable?

_____

_____

_____

What's your next action to make progress?

_____

_____

_____

What's your next date to review?

_____

_____

_____

WEEK 6 Get Accountability

Now that you've defined the areas you want to work on, you should pull together your accountability group. This should be a group of people you know and trust to provide you with objective feedback and to keep you accountable.

STEP 1: Decide Who Will Be in the Group

NAME	RELATIONSHIP TO YOU	WHAT PERSPECTIVE WILL THEY BRING?

STEP 2: Determine the Ground Rules

When and how often will you meet?

_____

_____

_____

For how long?

_____

_____

_____

What's on the agenda?

_____

_____

_____

What specifically are you looking for from them?

_____

_____

_____

What specifically are you not looking for from them?

_____

_____

_____

Step 3: Review Your Meetings

MEETING DATE	WHAT WORKED WELL?	WHAT WOULD YOU DO DIFFERENTLY?	WHAT DID YOU LEARN?	WHAT ARE YOUR NEXT ACTIONS?

WEEKS 7–14 Practice

By now you've built your accountability group and they're ready and willing to help. Now it's time to get to work. For the next eight weeks (weeks 7–14), you're going to be working on the specific areas you identified in your road map.

Each week, you're going to look for a specific occasion or event to practice one of the leadership disciplines and work through the process outlined in that chapter.

WEEK 7

What's the opportunity?

_____

_____

_____

What's your ideal outcome?

_____

_____

_____

Plan your approach.

_____

_____

_____

_____

_____

_____

What worked well?

_____

_____

What should you do differently next time?

_____

_____

_____

WEEK 8

What's the opportunity?

_____

_____

_____

What's your ideal outcome?

_____

_____

_____

Plan your approach.

_____

_____

_____

_____

_____

_____

What worked well?

_____

_____

What should you do differently next time?

_____

_____

_____

WEEK 9

What's the opportunity?

_____

_____

_____

What's your ideal outcome?

_____

_____

_____

Plan your approach.

_____

_____

_____

_____

_____

_____

What worked well?

_____

_____

What should you do differently next time?

_____

_____

_____

WEEK 10

What's the opportunity?

_____

_____

_____

What's your ideal outcome?

_____

_____

_____

Plan your approach.

_____

_____

_____

_____

_____

What worked well?

_____

_____

What should you do differently next time?

_____

_____

_____

WEEK 11

What's the opportunity?

_____

_____

_____

What's your ideal outcome?

_____

_____

_____

Plan your approach.

_____

_____

_____

_____

_____

What worked well?

_____

_____

What should you do differently next time?

_____

_____

_____

WEEK 12

What's the opportunity?

_____

_____

_____

What's your ideal outcome?

_____

_____

_____

Plan your approach.

_____

_____

_____

_____

_____

What worked well?

_____

_____

What should you do differently next time?

_____

_____

_____

WEEK 13

What's the opportunity?

_____

_____

_____

What's your ideal outcome?

_____

_____

_____

Plan your approach.

_____

_____

_____

_____

_____

What worked well?

_____

_____

What should you do differently next time?

_____

_____

_____

WEEK 14

What's the opportunity?

_____

_____

_____

What's your ideal outcome?

_____

_____

_____

Plan your approach.

_____

_____

_____

_____

_____

What worked well?

_____

_____

What should you do differently next time?

_____

_____

_____

WEEK 15 Review Your Progress

The final week, review your progress over the past fourteen weeks, and plan for another cycle of development.

1. Review your personal progress—take thirty minutes and walk through the following questions:

Did you achieve the goals you set for yourself in week 1?

_____

_____

_____

What worked well for you over the past fourteen weeks?

_____

_____

_____

What would you do differently?

_____

_____

_____

What did you learn about yourself?

_____

_____

_____

What areas would you like to continue to work on?

_____

_____

_____

How might you best do that?

_____

_____

_____

2. Review progress with your accountability group—spend fif-teen minutes with your accountability group and ask them the following questions:

In what areas have you seen improvement in my leadership?

_____

_____

_____

What areas do you feel I need to continue to work on?

_____

_____

_____

Where should I go next for support?

_____

_____

_____

Go to the webpage below for a video summary of this chapter and other exclusive resources:

Selfevolvedleader.com/Chapter-11

12

Toward a Self-Evolved Organization

The jazz musician and composer Charles Mingus once said, "You can't improvise on nothing. You gotta improvise on something." What I love most about jazz music is the interplay between musicians, their desire to try new things, and the knowledge that if you get a group of people in a room who know how to play their instrument, art can be made at any time. Yet as Mingus noted, all this is founded on a common set of beats, notes, and keys. No matter how many sax solos or drum riffs you go off on, there's always this shared beat, shared rhythm, and shared groove chugging along, something you can always return to. Organizations that build Self-Evolved Leadership into their core have the same ability to do great things, to push the boundaries, to create art. At their foundation, instead of the chaos of everyone trying to improvise at exactly the same time, there's a common beat, a common pulse, a common vision that sits under it all.

Back in the Introduction, I wrote that my ultimate goal for this book is to help entire organizations adopt a new approach to leadership—one that focuses more on the individual, puts compassion and empathy at the core, and ultimately gets better results than leadership strategies guided by the no-longer-useful elements of industrial-era management.

Like any revolution, the movement has to start at the bottom, with leaders who are fed up trying to juggle the many competing demands of their complex environment and being asked to produce miracles over and over again. You, dear reader, are that bastion, that light and that hope. What you do with the lessons from this book will go a long way toward dramatically increasing your own leadership effectiveness. But why stop there? Why not push on and aim to make a bigger difference in your department, your division, or your organization? Why not let the possibility of a new way of leading subsume every corner of your office, your plant, your campus?

For those leaders looking to make a bigger and bolder difference, here are some things you can try.

Building a Shared Vocabulary

The origins of the spoken word started some 30,000 to 100,000 years ago and gave *Homo sapiens* a competitive advantage over the other species around them. Instead of gesturing and grunting at each other, they were able to agree on a common set of verbal signals to direct and communicate their behavior. It's much easier to hunt, gather, and protect yourself when you can specifically call out prey, predators, and inclement weather.

Building great leadership across an organization is no different. In this oversaturated world of leadership models, theories, and gurus, it's no wonder our leaders are unsure of what we require of them. Those organizations that display exemplary leadership across the board have a common set of definitions and vocabulary that means the same thing no matter what part of the organization it's used in, yet the language remains flexible enough for individuals to still impart their own uniqueness.

If you're hoping to move toward a Self-Evolved organization, there are many terms and definitions in this book that would be helpful. If you can integrate all of them into a shared vocabulary, that's great! At a minimum, I would suggest integrating the following words and phrases into your leadership vernacular, most of which you want to encourage, but some you need to avoid.

Heroic leadership:
The problematic desire to lead by making diving catches, saving the day, and stealing victory from the jaws of defeat. Characterized by a leader's belief that their value comes from knowing the answers and working on the functional aspects of the role. Fun to watch but breeds learned helplessness in the team and burnout in the leader.

Learned helplessness:
A sense of resignation that when a problem or challenge occurs, the first and most obvious thing to do is to leave the problem at the foot of your manager or boss rather than tackle it yourself.

The Self-Evolved Leader:
One who understands that their job is to help their team achieve their common goals and, in doing so, help their people become the best versions of themselves.

Vision:
A simple statement that describes the future state of a team. To be used as a North Star for decision making and a clarion call to achieve something greater than the team itself.

Pulse:

A series of interactions that allows you to shift your vantage point as a leader and stay focused on achieving your vision. A way to plan in the time to focus on the important rather than the urgent.

Disciplines:

Six meta practices and five core practices that help you successfully navigate your implementation pulse and achieve your team vision. A set of skills and practices that, taken together, will help you achieve the Self-Evolved Leader's mantra.

Reclaiming your attention:

Protecting your headspace to give you more time to focus on the important things you need to work on rather than getting sucked into the urgent.

Facilitating team flow:

Managing the inputs to, around, and out from your team in a way that keeps you focused on achieving your current goals and at the same time develops each member.

Supporting high performance:

Helping your people discover the root cause of their issues, so they can assess the options in front of them by themselves. Then, encouraging them to devise a plan of action and backing their decision.

Having symbiotic conversations:

Having conversations that allow all parties the freedom to express their reality without fear of judgment. The focus should be to find the best outcome for the team as a whole and for the individuals within it, and the conversation will conclude with a clear next action that empowers people to opt in and supports those who choose to opt out.

Building shared accountability:
Building the environment that allows your team to set, achieve, and celebrate their collective goals.

Aligning Visions across the Organization

As more of the teams in your organization map out their vision, you may need to do some work to stitch them together. Doing this exercise usually shines a light on two aspects. The first is the quality and strength of your overarching organizational vision. You'll quickly learn whether that vision is weak or outdated if the individual team visions outstrip its usefulness and the level of enthusiasm surrounding it.

If that happens, then simply walk through a version of the process outlined in Chapter 3 with your most senior team. By this stage you'll likely have a number of team visions to use as input to your process and will emerge with something far stronger and more useful than you had before.

The second thing you'll need to do is ensure that the individual visions of each of your teams add up to the achievement of the overall vision. The best way to do this is to gather your leaders together, walk through each team vision, and talk through the following questions:

- What are the direct links between your team's vision and the organizational vision?

- In what ways might there be a disconnect between your team's vision and the organization's vision?

- What other team visions support or are supported by yours?

- What other team visions run the risk of competing with yours?

Finally, it can be helpful to make available and highlight each of the team visions across the organization. This gives those who may not normally work with each other the opportunity to get some insight into what's happening in other parts of the business.

Creating a Shared Pulse

Where I see many leaders go off the rails in this process is in not adhering to the implementation rhythm they create for themselves. What often happens is the first crisis derails whatever meeting it is that's scheduled for that day. Then, like a dieter who misses a gym session, they talk themselves out of the next one, and then the next one. Before you know it, the whole schedule has been blown up.

If you create the expectation of a shared pulse—all quarterly reviews happen the last week of the quarter, all monthly reviews the last Thursday of the month, for instance—it's much easier for everyone to stick to the rhythm. Second, you'll notice that the organization gets into a more predictable ebb and flow of strategic planning and execution as all teams go through a similar cycle.

A Collective Focus on Mastering the Disciplines

Over the course of a year, take each of the disciplines and spend two months to focus on them. Work through the approach from this book, and set up communities of practice that meet once every few weeks to give participants the opportunity to share their challenges and learn from each other. Provide the opportunity for everyone in your organization to share their goals for that two-month period and to share their personal success.

Go Deeper on Your Journey

Finally, if you'd like to take a deeper journey in making the transition to a Self-Evolved Leader or Organization, then I'd love to help. My own particular vision is that the tactics in this book will be used by organizations of all sizes, in all industries on every continent, in order to create a global body of individuals who lead with authenticity, purpose, and effectiveness. It's a lifelong goal and something I hope to be working on for many years to come.

To that end, there are four specific ways in which I may help you further.

Self-Evolved Leaders Resources

Get access to a range of online resources to help in your own leadership journey. You'll discover videos, blog articles, worksheets, exercises, and podcast episodes that will help you take the lessons here and incorporate them into your everyday leadership.

Selfevolvedleader.com/resources

Self-Paced Leadership Mastery Program

A fifteen-week online program designed to walk you step-by-step through your personal journey to Self-Evolved Leadership. Get weekly video tips and downloads to accelerate your evolution and access our Leadership Mastery community for peer learning and support.

Selfevolvedleader.com/mastery

Self-Evolved Leader Public Workshops

Join me for a one-day workshop in sunny Southern California to build your vision, pulse, and disciplines. Over the course of the day you'll get advice, guidance, and coaching on becoming a Self-Evolved Leader directly from me. This workshop is held four times a year and is limited in size to maximize our time and peer learning opportunities.

Selfevolvedleader.com/public

Self-Evolved Team In-House Workshop

Looking to bring these Self-Evolved Leadership principles to your team? This one-and-a-half-day workshop for up to twenty-five people can be held in or near your offices and will walk participants through the process of building a collective vision and pulse and provide hands-on guidance and support for developing the five core disciplines. Based on availability and location.

Selfevolvedleader.com/workshop

The Rest Is Up to You

In reading this book, you've already taken a huge step toward becoming a Self-Evolved Leader. The rest is up to you. You may not be able to control what happens in your organization or how your team reacts to your efforts, but you can control your response. Stay true to the desire to grow and develop as a leader, keep pushing for better, keep striving for excellence and resist mediocrity, and I hope I'll see you again at some point along your journey.

Go to the webpage below for a video summary of this chapter and other exclusive resources:

Selfevolvedleader.com/Chapter-12

Index

About the Author

D ave McKeown is the CEO of Outfield Leadership where he speaks, coaches, and trains on building leadership excellence at every level of an organization. He has a wealth of experience in connecting individual and team performance to improved business results with a particular focus on fast-growing, complex organizations. Originally from Northern Ireland, Dave traded the rain for sunshine and now lives in Southern California with his wonderful wife, Paris, and awesome Staffie, Maggie.

ENJOYED THIS BOOK?
I'D LOVE TO HEAR FROM YOU.

I truly hope you've gotten a lot out of this book. Feel free to let me know your thoughts at **dave@selfevolvedleader.com**, connect with me on Twitter **@davemckeown,** or even better, leave a review for it on Amazon.